Modern Lopi

NEW APPROACHES TO AN ICELANDIC CLASSIC

One

Lars Rains

PHOTOGRAPHY BY GALE ZUCKER

Modern Lopi: One

ISBN 13 (hardcover): 978-0-9970004-1-2
ISBN 13 (paperback): 978-0-9970004-2-9
ISBN 13 (e-book): 978-0-9970004-0-5

Technical Editor: Eleanor Dixon
Charts and Schematics: Andi Smith
Book Design and Layout: Elizabeth Green
Models: Toby Roxane Barna, Jack Hobbs, and Ariana McLean

Every effort has been made to ensure that all the information in this book is accurate at the time of publication.

If you have questions or comments about this book, or need information about licensing, custom editions, special sales, or academic/corporate purchases, please contact info@modernlopi.com

THIS BOOK IS DEDICATED TO VÉDÍS JÓNSDÓTTIR.

Thank you for the many years of colorful inspiration.

IN MEMORIAM

Joan Monsina Rains (1936-2014)

Contents

ASYMPTOTE 12

CLAPPING MUSIC 32

GIMLI 38

KATLA 70

HORNSTRANDIR 84

WINTER BLUEBERRIES 88

INTRODUCTION ■ 7
ABBREVIATIONS ■ 120
SPECIAL TECHNIQUES ■ 121
ABOUT THE AUTHOR ■ 127

HILDUR ■ 48

RÚNTUR ■ 58

WESTFJORDS ■ 98

MONSINA ■ 104

Introduction

It has been over twenty years since I first set foot inside my first yarn store, The Wool Mill in Toronto.

At the time, I had no idea that Wendy Mortimer would be starting me on an adventure that would so completely define my identity as an adult. I walked in, took some lessons and then proceeded to start on my very first project: a textured, two-toned Lopi cardigan out of Ístex Book 10. I had no idea that you weren't supposed to start with something so complicated; I just figured that all I had to do was follow the instructions and I'd be fine. Along the way, I learned that you probably shouldn't wrap the colorwork strands so tightly and that you should really try to follow the shaping directions exactly and not finish the pattern repeat first. I ended up with something that would fit someone four sizes smaller than me with shoulder pads that wouldn't have looked out of place in the previous decade.

Nevertheless, I persevered and kept knitting. One of my next projects was a blanket that I knit while watching the 1994 Lillehammer Olympics.

I guess that it could be considered my very first design, although I didn't think about it like that at the time. It consisted simply of thirteen stripes, one in each color of the Álafosslopi that was in stock at the store. The instructions for it would be very simple: cast on as many stitches as you can fit onto the longest needles you can find and knit until you run out of yarn. I can't tell you how heavy that blanket was at the end, but I can tell you that I had fallen in love with the subtle colors that the yarn came in, as well as the bold minimalism that I had stumbled upon with this design. I eventually framed it before my dogs chewed a hole in the center of it instead of just at the corners, and I still have it hanging over our king-size bed to this day.

To me, simplicity has always been the hallmark of traditional Icelandic pullovers.

In terms of construction, they are some of the easiest types of sweaters to work. Usually knit from the bottom up, the body is nothing more than a tube that is connected at the yoke to the sleeves. Decreases are worked over the course of the yoke until the stitches are bound off at the neck. The only seaming that needs to be done is at each underarm, where either live stitches are grafted or bound-off stitches are sewn together. If someone is looking to knit a first sweater, I almost always suggest that he or she start with a *lopapeysa*. This, of course, has nothing to do with my desire to introduce them to the wonders of Icelandic wool.

Icelandic sheep were first brought to the island by Viking settlers more than a thousand years ago. Like most Icelanders, they are described by Clara Parkes as being "bright, feisty, and independent" in *The Knitter's Book of Wool*. These animals are unusual in that they have two distinct coats. The outer layer or *tog* consists of long, smooth fibers, whereas the inner layer or *thel* is made up of shorter, softer fibers. When combined, they produce a yarn that is both highly insulating and water-repellant. Lopi often gets a bad reputation as a wool that is too scratchy and itchy when worn next to the skin. However, there is nothing like it to protect you from the elements on a cold winter's day.

When I lived in Canada, I would think nothing of throwing on an Icelandic sweater and venturing out into the frigid temperatures without a winter coat. Most of my first designs were knit using the bulkier Álafosslopi. After moving to New York City to pursue a doctorate in music theory, I found that the warmer climate severely restricted my ability to walk around in these sweaters. I have since started designing primarily with the worsted Léttlopi alternative, but I still find time to explore the possibilities inherent in all four commercial weights currently available in North America. In fact, this book is internally organized into four sections based on these different weights of yarn.

The first section features two designs in Léttlopi. The sweater, Asymptote, is a pullover with a traditional yoke design. Icelandic yokes look like they would be easy to create, but trust me, they aren't. It is very simple to stack horizontal bands on top of each other and call them a yoke design. The most amazing patterns have what I call a vertical flow to them, and I was so happy when I finally came up with this design. I also wanted to go with bold color combinations in this sweater. Just because something is traditional doesn't mean you can't make it a little more modern. The hat, Clapping Music, is a design that was inspired by my many years of studying twentieth-century music. I thought that the composition upon which it is based would lend itself very well to an arrangement for knitting needles and wool. For some reason, I love how this hat looks inside out.

The second section consists of four sweaters made out of Álafosslopi. Gimli is a men's pullover that features bright colors around the neck, an extended yoke depth and four rearrangements of a basic checkerboard pattern. Hildur is designed for women, with its subtle waist shaping and brightly colored Fair Isle patterns. Rúntur is more of a conceptual design for women, which explores connecting pattern bands across negative space and the use of reversed yokes. Katla is a monochromatic study in texture and construction through the use of saddle shoulders and extensive cabling. In each of these sweaters, I wanted to push the boundaries of what could be accomplished with Icelandic wool. They reflect some of my earliest attempts at sweater design, where I was more interested in coming up with one-of-a-kind art pieces rather than commercial patterns.

The third section contains two projects made out of Bulkylopi, the thickest wool in the Ístex family. The first, Hornstrandir, is a rectangular scarf consisting of basketweave squares in different sizes, which combine to create the impression of swirling ocean currents under the view of an imposing glacier. The second, Winter Blueberries, is an Estonian lace shawl worked in the largest weight of Icelandic yarn currently available. A traditional motif made up of simplified nupps is partially obscured by the use of one of the few variegated yarns put out by Ístex. In both cases, the bulky yarn works up quickly to produce accessories that will keep you all warm and snuggly when it is cold outside.

The fourth and final section comprises two projects as well, this time worked in Einband, the laceweight version of Icelandic wool produced by Ístex. Westfjords is a slouchy hat that features gradient stripes worked on teeny, tiny needles. (You tend to notice these things when you are used to knitting up Icelandic sweaters with much larger needles.) Monsina is a pullover made up of stacks of brightly colored Fair Isle motifs, with striped sleeves derived from the background colors in the yoke. By combining two strands of the Einband together, I was able to develop a sportweight alternative that works up relatively quickly.

I was always excited when a new book of Lopi patterns would come out each year. I would spend hours examining the color combinations and analyzing any new approaches to sweater construction within its pages.

Over the years, however, I began to realize that I had my own distinct aesthetic and voice as a designer that I wanted to share with others. Publishing a book by yourself is a long and intense process, but fortunately I have had a lot of help along the way. First and foremost, I would like to thank Linda Pratt of Westminster Fibers and Hulda Hákonardóttir of Ístex for their generous yarn support. I truly appreciate the trust that you have placed in me with this project. Linda, in particular, was the first person to have ever introduced me as a Lopi designer and I owe her a debt of gratitude for welcoming me into the knitting industry with such open arms. Trisha Malcolm and Carla Scott of Soho Publishing have also been wonderful mentors to me as I begin to navigate the waters as a knitwear designer.

You are only as good as the people you work with, and I was extremely fortunate to surround myself with some amazing professionals on my first book. Elizabeth Green might as well have been listed as the editor of this project, instead of simply doing the book layout. She held my hand during each stage of this process and patiently explained how books are published. She also gave me a good kick in the pants whenever she thought that I needed one. "Thank you!" doesn't even come close to saying how much I appreciate everything that you have done for me. My photographer, Gale Zucker, made all of my knitting projects look like they belonged on a runway. I had no idea how much work went into a professional shoot, from the styling and location prep to model wrangling and photo editing. Thank you so much for taking care of all of this for me. We had such a fun day on set despite the hot and humid weather.

I am so lucky to have a technical editor like Eleanor Dixon, who not only makes my patterns read better but also teaches me something new about communicating knitting ideas and concepts each time I work with her. I wouldn't have been able to include such beautiful charts and schematics in this book without the help and advice provided by Andi Smith. She also made me laugh at the times when I needed to the most during this long and exhausting process. Sarah Eyre was a gracious copy editor, helping to turn my pedantic prose into something worthy of appearing on the pages of a book. I must also express my gratitude to Ragnheiður Haralds- og Eiríksdóttir for her assistance with all things Icelandic. I would like to thank Toby Roxane Barna, Jack Hobbs and Ariana McLean for being my gorgeous models; as well as Yliana Tibitoski for her styling expertise and Deanna Nickel for her hair and make-up skills. Ashley Coates was also instrumental in working on my branding and graphic design in the very beginning. In addition, I am very grateful to Penny Shima Glanz for her assistance with setting up my website; Jocelyn Grayson for her marketing acumen; as well as PJ Lainis for knitting up a book sample on short notice; Jeremy Congdon, Shelley Hermanson and Rob Strauss for their test knitting; and Addie Betts for her many years of production knitting for me.

I have been fortunate to have had so many friends and supporters along for this ride. I want to thank Shannon Okey and the entire Cooperative Press family for finding ways to entertain me while I was procrastinating on Facebook; Ann Falcone, Kathleen Kollar and my Thursday night crew at the Village Knitter for giving me a place to go when I needed to get out of the house; Tara Swiger and my fellow Starship captains for freely sharing their business advice and keeping me accountable every week; Amy and Rena Nowacoski, Melanie Weiss and the rest of my Sunday afternoon group at Panera for their wacky shenanigans; Joe Wilcox and the men at the Spring Knitting retreat for providing me with a safe space to share my progress; Beth Brown-Reinsel, Gudrun Johnston, Mary Jane Mucklestone and all of the other designers at the Seyon Lodge retreat for continuing to inspire me and, more importantly, understanding what I was going through in trying to get this book out; as well as Jack Phillip Burwell, John Crane, Loraine Guritzky, Karen Hermann, Angela Monserrate, Betty Murphy, Ted Myatt, Brady Robinder, Hayes Russock, Mark Schuyler and Lou Simon for being the best knitting friends a guy could ever have.

Finally, I want to express my most heartfelt thanks to my family for all of their love and for believing in me even when I didn't believe in myself. I want to acknowledge my mother, Joan Monsina Rains, my sister, Wanda Leigh Rains and my sisters-in-law, Catherine Messina and Valerie Lotardo, for always being available when I needed to talk on the phone; as well as my mother-in-law, Lillian Oddo, for her constant encouragement and financial support. Last, but not least, I want to let everyone know just how much my husband, Monte Oddo, means to me. I wouldn't have been able to have finished this book without you and your unconditional love.

—Lars Rains, November 2015

Asymptote

Asymptote takes its name from analytic geometry, where an asymptote of a function is an imaginary line towards which the function gets closer, but never reaches, as it approaches infinity. I wanted to create a traditional Icelandic pullover with a yoke design that had strong, vertical movement. After making several swatches, I realized that the yoke I was striving for resembled one of the many graphs that I had drawn in my college math classes.

I decided to choose three contrasting colors from the same color family and I was pleasantly surprised with how well this color scheme worked with the main color of the pullover. Any three monochromatic colors can be selected for this pattern, as long as the brightest color is used as Color B, in order to emphasize the vertical asymptotes in the yoke. The Chart 1 colorwork in the women's version differs from the men's version in order to de-emphasize horizontal lines around the lower body.

Project Overview (Men's Pullover)

SIZES

XS (S, M, L, XL, XXL) to fit chest circumference of 36" (40", 44", 48", 52", 56") [91.5 cm (101.5 cm, 112 cm, 122 cm, 132 cm, 142 cm)] with 2-3" [3-6 cm] of positive ease intended.

Shown in Size XL with 2" [3 cm] of positive ease.

FINISHED MEASUREMENTS

Chest Circumference: 39" (42", 46½", 51", 54", 58½") [97.5 cm (105 cm, 116.5 cm, 127.5 cm, 135 cm, 146.5 cm)].

Pullover Length: 27" (27¾", 28¼", 29¼", 29½", 30¼") [68 cm (69.5 cm, 71 cm, 74 cm, 74.5 cm, 76 cm)].

YARN

Ístex Léttlopi: 100% Icelandic wool; 109 yds [100 m] per 1.75 oz [50 g] skein.

- Color A: 0056 Light Ash Heather; 7 (8, 8, 9, 9, 10) skeins.
- Color B: 1406 Spring Green Heather; 2 (2, 2, 3, 3, 3) skeins.
- Color C: 1405 Bottle Green Heather; 1 skein for all sizes.
- Color D: 9421 Celery Green Heather; 1 (1, 2, 2, 2, 2) skein(s).

NEEDLES

US #8 [5.0 mm], or size needed to obtain gauge;

- All sizes: 24" [60 cm] and 32" [80 cm] circular needles.
- Sizes M-XXL: 40" [100 cm] circular needles.
- Sizes XL-XXL: 60" [150 cm] circular needles.
- Optional: double-pointed needles for small-circumference knitting.

US #6 [4.0 mm], or two sizes smaller than gauge needles;

- All sizes: 24" [60 cm] and 32" [80 cm] circular needles.
- Optional: double-pointed needles for small-circumference knitting.

Note: Work the body with the needle length closest to the finished chest measurement. Use the longest needles indicated for your size when joining the body and the sleeves together at the beginning of the yoke. Switch to shorter lengths as needed while working the yoke. Use your preferred method of small-circumference knitting to work the neckband and the sleeves.

NOTIONS

3 stitch markers (including one to indicate end of round).

4 stitch holders or waste yarn (to hold stitches at each underarm).

1 long and 2 short circular stitch holders or waste yarn (to hold live stitches for body and sleeves).

Blunt tapestry needle.
Blocking pins, if desired.

GAUGE

16 sts and 22 rnds = 4" [10 cm] in St st using larger needles, after blocking.

Construction Notes

This garment is worked seamlessly in the round from the bottom up.

Directions for the Channel Island Cast On, the Icelandic Bind Off, Short-Row Shaping Using Yarn Overs and the Kitchener Stitch, as well as other useful information, can be found in the Special Techniques section of the book.

The body is worked from the hem to the underarms in stockinette with stranded colorwork without shaping.

The sleeves are worked similarly from the cuff to the underarm and are shaped with paired, symmetrical increases.

The stitches for the body and both sleeves are joined together on one set of circular needles to work the yoke.

The underarm stitches are placed on stitch holders or waste yarn and are grafted together during the finishing process.

Short-Row shaping is worked at the shoulders to increase the back length of the garment.

1x1 Ribbing is always worked using the smaller needles.

Stitch Patterns

1X1 RIBBING

Worked over a multiple of 2 sts; 1-rnd repeat.
Rnd 1: *K1, p1; rep from * around.
Rep Rnd 1 as directed.

Pattern Instructions

BODY

With smaller needles and using Channel Island cast-on method, CO 156 (168,186, 204, 216, 234) sts using Color A. Join in the rnd and pm to indicate EOR, being careful not to twist sts. Work 1x1 Ribbing for 12 rnds and then knit 1 rnd.

Switch to larger needles and knit 1 rnd. Work Rnds 1-17 of Chart 1 with Colors A, B and C, repeating to EOR. Cut Colors B and C.

With Color A only, work in St st until body measures 15½" (16", 16", 16½", 16½", 17") [39.5 cm (40.5 cm, 40.5 cm, 42 cm, 42 cm, 43 cm)], or desired length to underarm.

Knit to 7 (8, 9, 10, 11, 12) sts before EOR marker. Place the next 14 (16, 18, 20, 22, 24) sts on stitch holder or waste yarn, removing marker. Place the rem 142 (152, 168, 184, 194, 210) sts on long circular stitch holder or waste yarn and set aside.

SLEEVES (MAKE 2)

With smaller needles, using preferred needles for small-circumference knitting and using Channel Island cast-on method, CO 46 (46, 48, 48, 50, 50) sts using Color A. Join in the rnd and pm to indicate EOR, being careful not to twist sts. Work 1x1 Ribbing for 12 rnds. Knit 1 rnd, inc 2 (2, 0, 0, 4, 4) sts evenly. 48 (48, 48, 48, 54, 54) sts on needles.

Switch to larger needles and knit 1 rnd. Work Rnds 1-17 of Chart 1 with Colors A, B and C, repeating to EOR. Cut Colors B and C.

With Color A only, work in St st and inc 1 st at beg and end of every 9th (7th, 6th, 5th, 5th, 5th) rnd, 7 (9, 11, 13, 13, 15) times. 62 (66, 70, 74, 80, 84) sts on needles.

Work in St st until sleeve measures 18¾" (19", 19½", 19½", 19¾", 20") [47.5 cm (48.5 cm, 49.5 cm, 49.5 cm, 50 cm, 51 cm)], or desired length to underarm.

Knit to 7 (8, 9, 10, 11, 12) sts before EOR marker. Place the next 14 (16, 18, 20, 22, 24) sts on stitch holder or waste yarn, removing marker. Place the rem 48 (50, 52, 54, 58, 60) sts on short circular stitch holder or waste yarn and set aside.

YOKE

With the longest larger needles, RS facing and using Color A, join body and sleeves together as follows:

Knit 48 (50, 52, 54, 58, 60) sts of first sleeve, pm, knit 64 (68, 75, 82, 86, 93) sts of body for front, pm. Place next 14 (16, 18, 20, 22,

24) sts of body on stitch holder or waste yarn. Knit 48 (50, 52, 54, 58, 60) sts of second sleeve, knit rem 64 (68, 75, 82, 86, 93) sts of body for back, pm to indicate EOR. 224 (236, 254, 272, 288, 306) sts on needles.

Knit 1 rnd, dec 0 (4, 6, 0, 0, 2) sts evenly. 224 (232, 248, 272, 288, 304) sts on needles. Knit 6 (6, 8, 9, 9, 9) rnds even.

Work Chart 2 with Colors A, B, C and D, repeating to EOR, skipping rnds and decreasing sts where indicated. 84 (87, 93, 102, 108, 114) sts on needles. Cut Colors B, C and D. With Color A only, knit 1 rnd, dec 8 (7, 7, 10, 12, 14) sts evenly. 76 (80, 86, 92, 96, 100) sts on needles.

Short Rows

Read the information on Short-Row Shaping Using Yarn Overs in the Special Techniques section of the book before proceeding. The remainder of the garment is worked in Color A only.

Short Row 1 (RS): Knit to first marker, turn and yo.

Short Row 2 (WS): Purl to EOR marker, sl m, purl to second marker, turn and yo.

Short Row 3: Knit to EOR marker, sl m, knit to 8 sts before first marker, turn and yo.

Short Row 4: Purl to EOR marker, sl m, purl to 8 sts before second marker, turn and yo.

Short Row 5: Knit to EOR marker, sl m, knit to 16 sts before first marker, turn and yo.

Short Row 6: Purl to EOR marker, sl m, purl to 16 sts before second marker, turn and yo.

Short Row 7: Knit across back to EOR marker. All short rows are completed.

Knit 1 rnd, working all short-row yarn overs together with adjacent sts to close gaps.

NECKBAND

Switch to smaller needles and knit 1 rnd. Work 1x1 Ribbing for 12 rnds. BO all sts loosely using Icelandic bind-off method.

FINISHING

Graft underarm sts together using Kitchener Stitch method. Weave in all loose ends with tapestry needle on the inside of the garment. Block to finished measurements.

Asymptote
Men's Pullover
Chart 1: Band Chart

Color Legend

- Knit with Color A: 0056 Light Ash Heather
- Knit with Color B: 1406 Spring Green Heather
- Knit with Color C: 1405 Bottle Green Heather

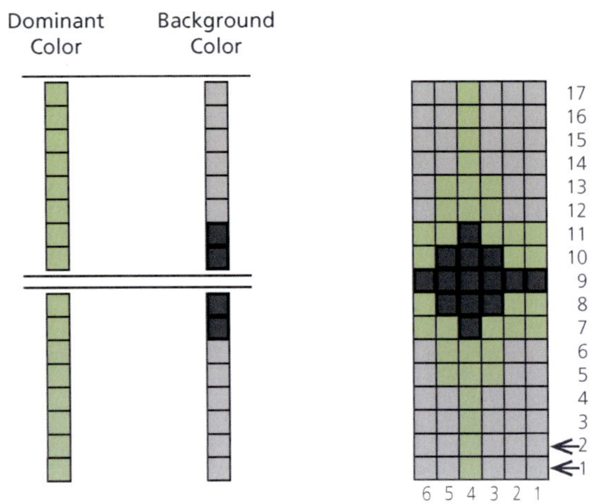

Asymptote
Men's Pullover
Chart 2: Yoke Chart

Color Legend

- Knit with Color A: 0056 Light Ash Heather
- Knit with Color B: 1406 Spring Green Heather
- Knit with Color C: 1405 Bottle Green Heather
- Knit with Color D: 9421 Celery Green Heather

Stitch Legend

- No Stitch
- K2tog with Color Indicated
- SSK with Color Indicated

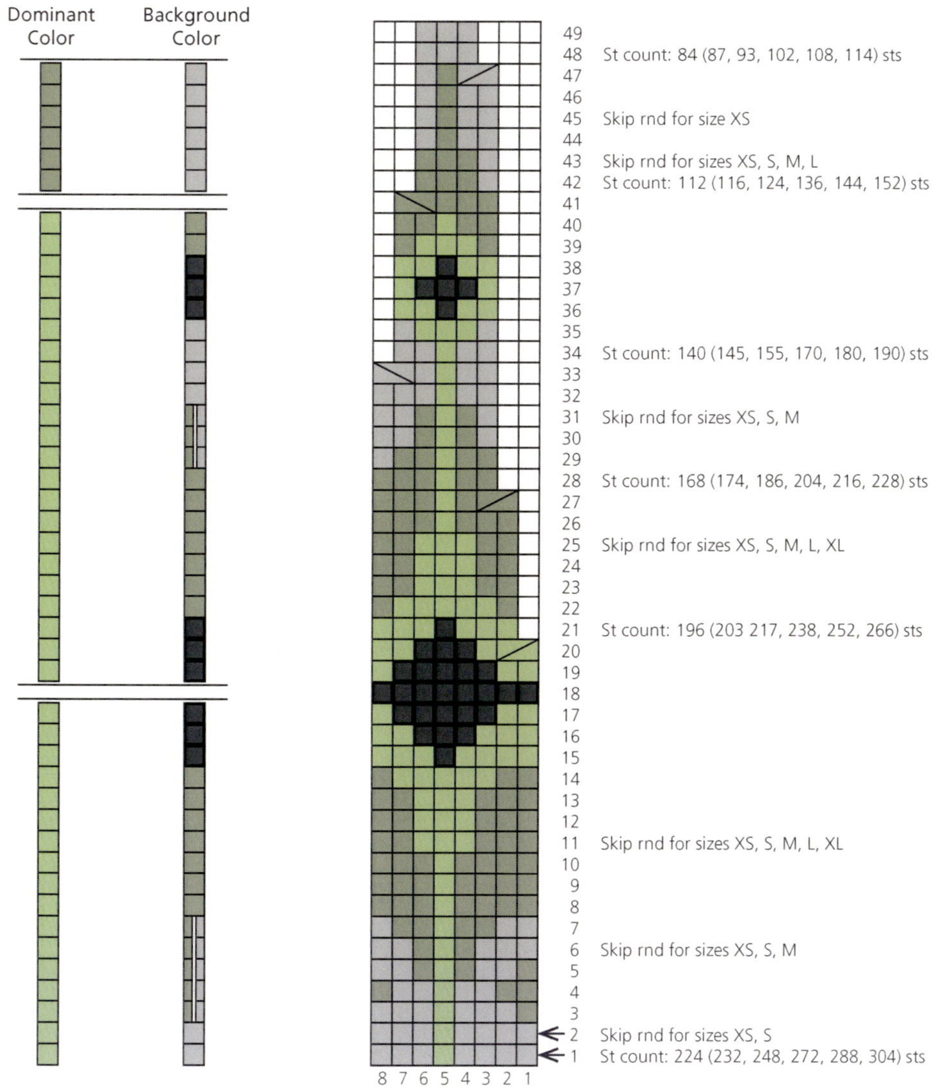

Asymptote Men's Pullover Schematic

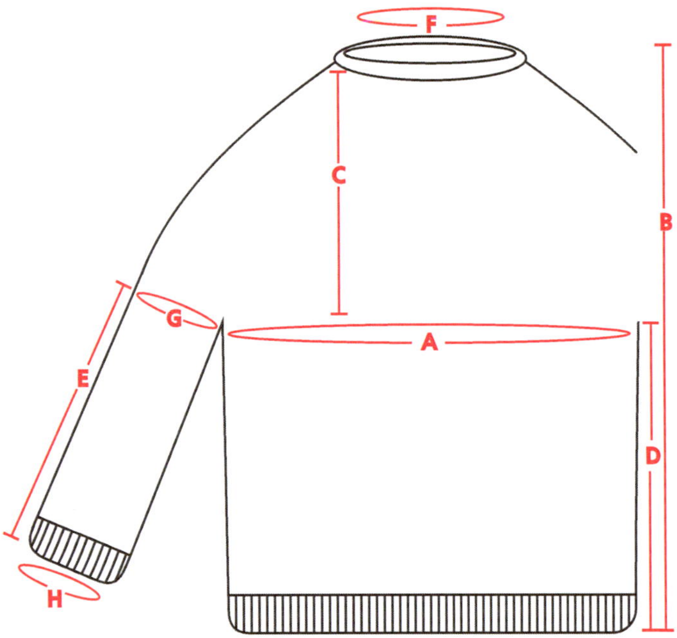

A CHEST CIRCUMFERENCE:
39 (42, 46½, 51, 54, 58½) inches
97.5 (105, 116.5, 127.5, 135, 146.5) cm

B PULLOVER LENGTH:
27 (27¾, 28¼, 29¼, 29½, 30¼) inches
68 (69.5, 71, 74, 74.5, 76) cm

C YOKE DEPTH:
9¼ (9½, 10, 10½, 10¾, 11) inches
23 (23.5, 25, 26.5, 27, 28) cm

D BODY LENGTH:
15½ (16, 16, 16½, 16½, 17) inches
39.5 (40.5, 40.5, 42, 42, 43) cm

E SLEEVE LENGTH:
18¾ (19, 19½, 19½, 19¾, 20) inches
47.5 (48.5, 49.5, 49.5, 50, 51) cm

F NECK CIRCUMFERENCE:
19 (20, 21½, 23, 24, 25) inches
47.5 (50, 54, 57.5, 60, 62.5) cm

G UPPER ARM CIRCUMFERENCE:
15½ (16½, 17½, 18½, 20, 21) inches
39 (41.5, 44, 46.5, 50, 53.5) cm

H CUFF CIRCUMFERENCE:
11½ (11½, 12, 12, 12½, 12½) inches
29 (29, 30, 30, 31.5, 31.5) cm

Asymptote (Women's Pullover)

Construction Notes

This garment is worked seamlessly in the round from the bottom up.

Directions for the Channel Island Cast On, the Icelandic Bind Off, Short-Row Shaping Using Yarn Overs and the Kitchener Stitch, as well as other useful information, can be found in the Special Techniques section of the book.

The body is worked from the hem to the underarms in stockinette with stranded colorwork without shaping.

The sleeves are worked similarly from the cuff to the underarm and are shaped with paired, symmetrical increases.

The stitches for the body and both sleeves are joined together on one set of circular needles to work the yoke.

The underarm stitches are placed on stitch holders or waste yarn and are grafted together during the finishing process.

Short-Row shaping is worked at the shoulders to increase the back length of the garment.

1x1 Ribbing is always worked using the smaller needles.

Stitch Patterns

1X1 RIBBING

Worked over a multiple of 2 sts; 1-rnd repeat.
Rnd 1: *K1, p1; rep from * around.
Rep Rnd 1 as directed.

Pattern Instructions

BODY

With smaller needles and using Channel Island cast-on method, CO 144 (162, 180, 192, 210, 228) sts using Color A. Join in the rnd and pm to indicate EOR, being careful not to twist sts. Work 1x1 Ribbing for 12 rnds and then knit 1 rnd.

Switch to larger needles and knit 1 rnd. Work Rnds 1-17 of Chart 1 with Colors A, B and C, repeating to EOR. Cut Colors B and C.

With Color A only, work in St st until body measures 14" (14", 14½", 14½", 15", 15") [35.5 cm (35.5 cm, 37 cm, 37 cm, 38 cm, 38 cm)], or desired length to underarm.

Knit to 7 (8, 9, 10, 11, 12) sts before EOR marker. Place the next 14 (16, 18, 20, 22, 24) sts on stitch holder or waste yarn, removing marker. Place the rem 130 (146, 162, 172, 188, 204) sts on long circular stitch holder or waste yarn and set aside.

SLEEVES (MAKE 2)

With smaller needles, using preferred needles for small-circumference knitting and using Channel Island cast-on method, CO 44 (44, 46, 46, 48, 48) sts using Color A. Join in the rnd and pm to indicate EOR, being

Project Overview (Women's Pullover)

SIZES

XS (S, M, L, XL, XXL) to fit bust circumference of 34" (38", 42", 46", 50", 54") [86.5 cm (96.5 cm, 106.5 cm, 117 cm, 127 cm, 137 cm)] with 2-3" [3-6 cm] of positive ease intended.

Shown in Size M with 3" [6 cm] of positive ease.

FINISHED MEASUREMENTS

Bust Circumference: 36" (40½", 45", 48", 52½", 57") [90 cm (101.5 cm, 112.5 cm, 120 cm, 131.5 cm, 142.5 cm)].

Pullover Length: 24¾" (25", 25½", 26", 26¾", 27") [62.5 cm (63 cm, 65 cm, 65.5 cm, 67 cm, 68 cm)].

YARN

Ístex Léttlopi: 100% Icelandic wool; 109 yds [100 m] per 1.75 oz [50 g] skein.

- Color A: 1413 Lilac Heather; 6 (7, 7, 8, 8, 9) skeins.
- Color B: 1408 Light Red Heather; 2 (2, 2, 3, 3, 3) skeins.
- Color C: 9417 Dark Wine; 1 skein for all sizes.
- Color D: 1412 Pink Heather; 1 (1, 2, 2, 2, 2) skein(s).

NEEDLES

US #8 [5.0 mm], or size needed to obtain gauge;

- All sizes: 24" [60 cm] and 32" [80 cm] circular needles.
- Sizes M-XXL: 40" [100 cm] circular needles.
- Sizes XL-XXL: 60" [150 cm] circular needles.
- Optional: double-pointed needles for small-circumference knitting.

US #6 [4.0 mm], or two sizes smaller than gauge needles;

- All sizes: 24" [60 cm] and 32" [80 cm] circular needles.
- Optional: double-pointed needles for small-circumference knitting.

Note: Work the body with the needle length closest to the finished bust measurement. Use the longest needles indicated for your size when joining the body and the sleeves together at the beginning of the yoke. Switch to shorter lengths as needed while working the yoke. Use your preferred method of small-circumference knitting to work the neckband and the sleeves.

NOTIONS

3 stitch markers (including one to indicate end of round).

4 stitch holders or waste yarn (to hold stitches at each underarm).

1 long and 2 short circular stitch holders or waste yarn (to hold live stitches for body and sleeves).

Blunt tapestry needle.
Blocking pins, if desired.

GAUGE

16 sts and 22 rnds = 4" [10 cm] in St st using larger needles, after blocking.

careful not to twist sts. Work 1x1 Ribbing for 12 rnds. Knit 1 rnd, inc 4 (4, 2, 2, 0, 0) sts evenly. 48 (48, 48, 48, 48, 48) sts on needles.

Switch to larger needles and knit 1 rnd. Work Rnds 1-17 of Chart 1 with Colors A, B and C, repeating to EOR. Cut Colors B and C.

With Color A only, work in St st and inc 1 st at beg and end of every 20th (12th, 8th, 6th, 5th, 4th) rnd, 3 (5, 8, 10, 13, 16) times. 54 (58, 64, 68, 74, 80) sts on needles.

Work in St st until sleeve measures 17½" (17¾", 18", 18¼", 18½", 18¾") [44.5 cm (45 cm, 46 cm, 46.5 cm, 47 cm, 47.5 cm)], or desired length to underarm.

Knit to 7 (8, 9, 10, 11, 12) sts before EOR marker. Place the next 14 (16, 18, 20, 22, 24) sts on stitch holder or waste yarn, removing marker. Place the rem 40 (42, 46, 48, 52, 56) sts on short circular stitch holder or waste yarn and set aside.

YOKE

With the longest larger needles, RS facing and using Color A, join body and sleeves together as follows:

Knit 40 (42, 46, 48, 52, 56) sts of first sleeve, pm, knit 58 (65, 72, 76, 83, 90) sts of body for front, pm. Place next 14 (16, 18, 20, 22, 24) sts of body on stitch holder or waste yarn. Knit 40 (42, 46, 48, 52, 56) sts of second sleeve, knit rem 58 (65, 72, 76, 83, 90) sts of body for back, pm to indicate EOR. 196 (214, 236, 248, 270, 292) sts on needles.

Knit 1 rnd, dec 4 (6, 4, 0, 6, 4) sts evenly. 192 (208, 232, 248, 264, 288) sts on needles. Knit 2 rnds even.

Work Chart 2 with Colors A, B, C and D, repeating to EOR, skipping rnds and decreasing sts where indicated. 72 (78, 87, 93, 99, 108) sts on needles. Cut Colors B, C and D. With Color A only, knit 1 rnd, dec 6 (6, 11, 11, 13, 18) sts evenly. 66 (72, 76, 82, 86, 90) sts on needles.

Short Rows

Read the information on Short-Row Shaping Using Yarn Overs in the Special Techniques section of the book before proceeding. The remainder of the garment is worked in Color A only.

Short Row 1 (RS): Knit to first marker, turn and yo.

Short Row 2 (WS): Purl to EOR marker, sl m, purl to second marker, turn and yo.

Short Row 3: Knit to EOR marker, sl m, knit to 8 sts before first marker, turn and yo.

Short Row 4: Purl to EOR marker, sl m, purl to 8 sts before second marker, turn and yo.

Short Row 5: Knit to EOR marker, sl m, knit to 16 sts before first marker, turn and yo.

Short Row 6: Purl to EOR marker, sl m, purl to 16 sts before second marker, turn and yo.

Short Row 7: Knit across back to EOR marker. All short rows are completed.

Knit 1 rnd, working all short-row yarn overs together with adjacent sts to close gaps.

NECKBAND

Switch to smaller needles and knit 1 rnd. Work 1x1 Ribbing for 24 rnds. BO all sts loosely using Icelandic bind-off method. Fold neckband in half and sew to the inside of the garment.

FINISHING

Graft underarm sts together using Kitchener Stitch method. Weave in all loose ends with tapestry needle on the inside of the garment. Block to finished measurements.

Asymptote Women's Pullover Chart 1: Band Chart

Color Legend

- Knit with Color A: 1413 Lilac Heather
- Knit with Color B: 1408 Light Red Heather
- Knit with Color C: 9417 Dark Wine

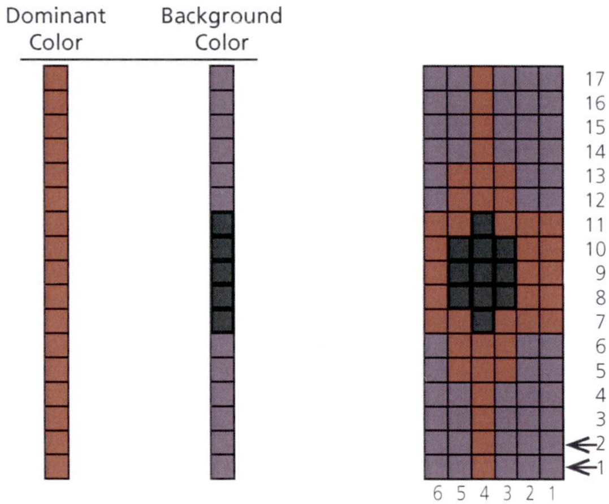

Asymptote Women's Pullover Chart 2: Yoke Chart

Color Legend

- Knit with Color A: 1413 Lilac Heather
- Knit with Color B: 1408 Light Red Heather
- Knit with Color C: 9417 Dark Wine
- Knit with Color D: 1412 Pink Heather

Stitch Legend

- No Stitch
- K2tog with Color Indicated
- SSK with Color Indicated

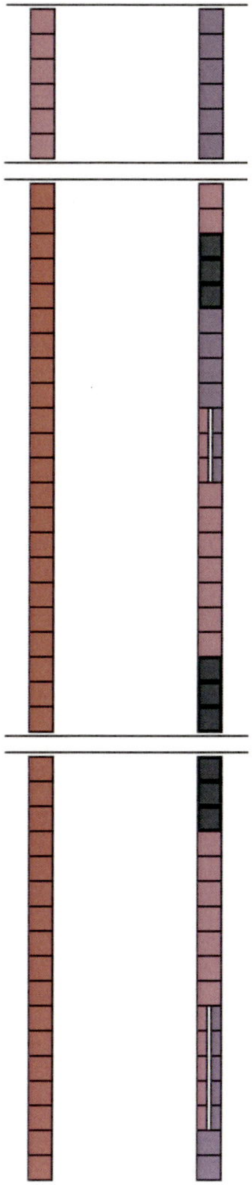

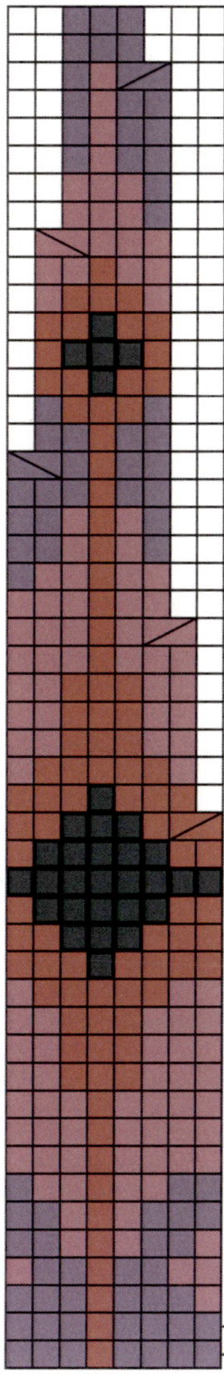

Asymptote Women's Pullover Schematic

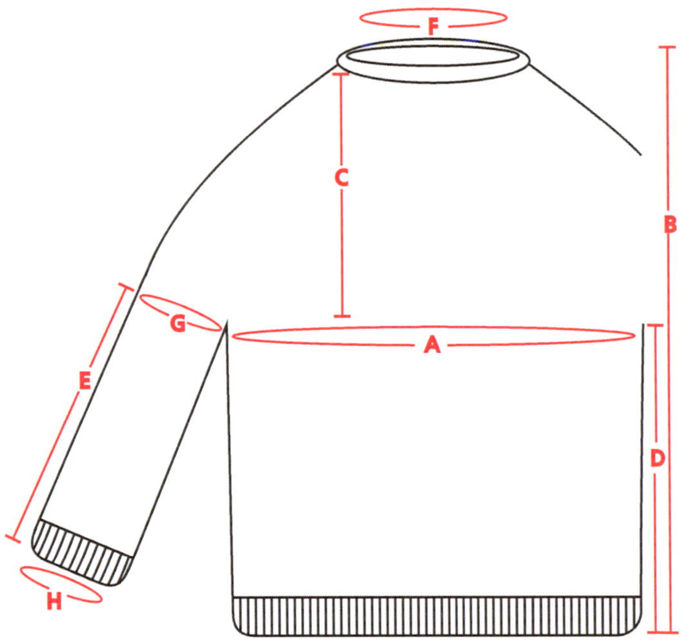

A BUST CIRCUMFERENCE:
36 (40½, 45, 48, 52½, 57) inches
90 (101.5, 112.5, 120, 131.5, 142.5) cm

B PULLOVER LENGTH:
24¾ (25, 25½, 26, 26¾, 27) inches
62.5 (63, 65, 65.5, 67, 68) cm

C YOKE DEPTH:
8½ (8¾, 9, 9¼, 9½, 9¾) inches
21.5 (22, 22.5, 23, 23.5, 24.5) cm

D BODY LENGTH:
14 (14, 14½, 14½, 15, 15) inches
35.5 (35.5, 37, 37, 38, 38) cm

E SLEEVE LENGTH:
17½ (17¾, 18, 18¼, 18½, 18¾) inches
44.5 (45, 46, 46.5, 47, 47.5) cm

F NECK CIRCUMFERENCE:
16½ (18, 19, 20½, 21½, 22½) inches
41.5 (45, 47.5, 51.5, 54, 56.5) cm

G UPPER ARM CIRCUMFERENCE:
13½ (14½, 16, 17, 18½, 20) inches
34 (36.5, 40, 42.5, 46.5, 50) cm

H CUFF CIRCUMFERENCE:
11 (11, 11½, 11½, 12, 12) inches
27.5 (27.5, 29, 29, 30, 30) cm

Clapping Music

Clapping Music is an early minimalist composition by Steve Reich in which two performers begin by clapping the same rhythmic pattern in unison. One part remains fixed throughout the entire performance, while the other part shifts forwards by one beat at regular intervals until both parts are once again in unison with each other. This project interprets knitting as a performative act and focuses more on the process than on the end result. It explores how this example of phase music could be realized visually as a functional and wearable piece of art without having any preconceived idea of what it would look like in the end.

In this pattern, phase shifts are introduced every three rows, with the fundamental rhythm incorporated as the middle row in order to demonstrate how each phase shift interacts with the stabilizing component of the performance. By arranging the composition in this manner, I was able to illustrate the relationships between the two parts as they come in and out of phase with each other, as well as the connections between the phase shifts themselves.

[CONTINUED ON PAGE 34]

Steve Reich says that "you learn the musical material of the piece and put the score aside because it is no longer necessary: it would only be a distraction. Everything is worked out, there is no improvisation, but the psychology of performance—what really happens when you play—is total involvement with the sound, total sensuous intellectual involvement." Once you understand how the knitting pattern is organized, you can stop worrying about how the project is going to turn out and begin to focus on the act of knitting itself. I hope you enjoy the performance!

Construction Notes

This hat is worked seamlessly in the round from the bottom up.

Directions for the Knitted Cast On, as well as other useful information, can be found in the Special Techniques section of the book.

Color A is the main color throughout the pattern; Color B is the contrasting color used only in Chart 1.

3x3 Ribbing is always worked using the smaller needles.

Stitch Patterns

3X3 RIBBING

Worked over a multiple of 6 sts; 1-rnd repeat.
Rnd 1: *K3, p3; rep from * around.
Rep Rnd 1 as directed.

Pattern Instructions

BRIM

With smaller needles and using Knitted cast-on method, CO 72 (84, 96) sts using Color A. Join in the rnd and pm to indicate EOR, being careful not to twist sts.

Work 3x3 Ribbing for 6 rnds.

BODY

With larger needles, knit 3 rnds. Work Rnds 1-39 of Chart 1 with Colors A and B, repeating to EOR. Cut Color B. With Color A only, knit 3 rnds.

CROWN

Work decreases as follows, switching to preferred needles for small-circumference knitting when necessary:

Size L only:
*K6, k2tog; rep from * around. 84 sts on needles.
Knit all sts.

Project Overview

SIZES

S (M, L) to fit head circumference of 18" (20", 22") [45.5 cm (51 cm, 56 cm)] with ¾-2" [2-5 cm] negative ease intended.

Shown in Size L with ¾" [2 cm] of negative ease.

FINISHED MEASUREMENTS

Head Circumference: 16" (18¾", 21¼") [40.5 cm (47.5 cm, 54 cm).

Height from Brim to Crown: 10" (10¼", 10¾") [25.5 cm (26 cm, 27.5 cm)].

YARN

Ístex Léttlopi: 100% Icelandic wool; 109 yds [100 m] per 1.75 oz [50 g] skein.

- Color A: 1403 Lapis Blue Heather; 1 skein for all sizes.
- Color B: 1406 Spring Green Heather; 1 skein for all sizes.

NEEDLES

US #8 [5.0 mm], or size needed to obtain gauge;

- All sizes: 16" [40 cm] circular needles.
- Optional: double-pointed needles for small-circumference knitting.

US #6 [4.0 mm], or two sizes smaller than gauge needles;

- All sizes: 16" [40 cm] circular needles.

Note: Begin with circular needles to accommodate the cast-on stitches for the brim. Use your preferred method of small-circumference knitting to work the crown.

NOTIONS

1 stitch marker (to indicate end of round).
Blunt tapestry needle.
Blocking pins, if desired.

GAUGE

18 sts and 24 rnds = 4" [10 cm] in stranded colorwork using larger needles, after blocking.

Sizes M and L only:
*K5, k2tog; rep from * around.
72 sts on needles.
Knit all sts.

All sizes:
*K4, k2tog; rep from * around.
60 sts on needles.
Knit all sts.

*K3, k2tog; rep from * around.
48 sts on needles.
Knit all sts.

*K2, k2tog; rep from * around.
36 sts on needles.
Knit all sts.

*K1, k2tog; rep from * around.
24 sts on needles.
Knit all sts.

*K2tog; rep from * around. 12 sts on needles.

Cut working yarn and pull tightly through rem sts.

FINISHING

Weave in all loose ends with tapestry needle on the inside of the hat. Block to finished measurements.

Clapping Music Unisex Hat
Chart 1: Body Chart

Color Legend

- Knit with Color A: 1403 Lapis Blue Heather
- Knit with Color B: 1406 Spring Green Heather

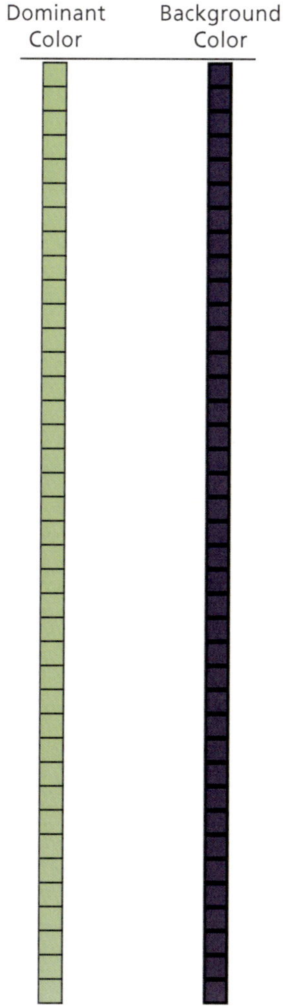

Gimli

Gimli is named after a small town in Manitoba where an annual Icelandic festival is held. It is the cultural center of New Iceland, where so many Icelanders, like my great-grandmother, settled after arriving in Canada. I convinced my twin sister to accompany me to the festival on a recent trip back home and we spent a wonderful weekend immersing ourselves in Icelandic traditions.

While we were there, I stumbled upon the last few skeins anywhere of Álafosslopi in my favorite color: 0014 Forest Heather. Sadly, it is only available now as Plötulopi or pencil roving, which is much harder to acquire. I set out to create a horizontal yoke design that explored the different ways that a checkerboard motif could be worked using only three colors. My prototype (shown on Page 7) featured an oversized ribbed neckband that could be rolled up to cover my face and a much deeper yoke than usual, which provided a surprisingly comfortable fit. The version of the pullover presented here maintains these features, while updating the colors and reversing the order of the horizontal bands of the original.

Project Overview

SIZES

XS (S, M, L, XL, XXL) to fit chest circumference of 36" (40", 44", 48", 52", 56") [91.5 cm (101.5 cm, 112 cm, 122 cm, 132 cm, 142 cm)] with 3-3¾" [5.5-8 cm] of positive ease intended.

Shown in Men's Size M with 3" [5.5 cm] of positive ease.

FINISHED MEASUREMENTS

Chest Circumference: 39½" (43¾", 47", 51¼", 55½", 59¾") [98.5 cm (109.5 cm, 117.5 cm, 128 cm, 138.5 cm, 149.5 cm)].

Pullover Length: 27¾" (28¼", 29¼", 30½", 31¼", 31¾") [69.5 cm (71 cm, 73.5 cm, 76.5 cm, 78.5 cm, 80 cm)].

YARN

Ístex Álafosslopi: 100% Icelandic wool; 109 yds [100 m] per 3.5 oz [100 g] skein.

- Color A: 1240 Dark Magenta; 2 (2, 2, 3, 3, 3) skeins.
- Color B: 0051 White; 1 (1, 1, 2, 2, 2) skein(s).
- Color C: 9967 Teal Heather; 6 (6, 7, 7, 8, 8) skeins.

NEEDLES

US #10 [6.0 mm], or size needed to obtain gauge;

- All sizes: 24" [60 cm] and 32" [80 cm] circular needles.
- Sizes M-XXL: 40" [100 cm] circular needles.
- Sizes XL-XXL: 60" [150 cm] circular needles.
- Optional: double-pointed needles for small-circumference knitting.

US #8 [5.0 mm], or two sizes smaller than gauge needles;

- All sizes: 24" [60 cm] and 32" [80 cm] circular needles.
- Optional: double-pointed needles for small-circumference knitting.

Note: Begin with the shortest circular needles and switch to longer lengths as needed while working the yoke. Use your preferred method of small-circumference knitting to work the neckband and the sleeves.

NOTIONS

1 stitch marker (to indicate end of round).

2 short, circular stitch holders or waste yarn (to hold live stitches for sleeve).

Blunt tapestry needle.
Blocking pins, if desired.

GAUGE

15 sts and 20 rnds = 4" [10 cm] in St st using larger needles, after blocking.

Construction Notes

This garment is worked seamlessly in the round from the top down.

Directions for the Knitted Cast On and the Icelandic Bind Off, as well as other useful information, can be found in the Special Techniques section of the book.

The neckband is worked first, then the yoke is knit in the round with increases occurring before and after each band of stranded colorwork.

The yoke is then divided to work the body, with additional stitches cast on at the underarms, while the sleeve stitches are held separately.

The sleeves are worked from the upper arm down with stitches picked up from the cast-on edge at the underarms and are tapered with decreases to the cuff.

2x2 Ribbing is always worked using the smaller needles.

Stitch Patterns

2X2 RIBBING

Worked over a multiple of 4 sts; 1-rnd repeat.
Rnd 1: *K2, p2; rep from * around.
Rep Rnd 1 as directed.

Pattern Instructions

NECKBAND

With smaller needles and using Knitted cast-on method, CO 56 (60, 64, 68, 72, 76) sts using Color A. Knit 1 row. Join in the rnd and pm to indicate EOR, being careful not to twist sts. Work 2x2 Ribbing for 2 rnds. Cut Color A. Join Color B and work 2x2 Ribbing for 3 rnds. Cut Color B. Join Color C and work 2x2 Ribbing for 6 rnds.

Switch to larger needles and work Inc Rnd 1: *K2, M1; rep from * around. 84 (90, 96, 102, 108, 114) sts on needles. Knit 13 rnds.

Work Inc Rnd 2: *K2, M1; rep from * around. 126 (135, 144, 153, 162, 171) sts on needles. Knit 1 rnd even. Knit 1 rnd, inc 0 (3, 0, 3, 0, 3) sts evenly. 126 (138, 144, 156, 162, 174) sts on needles. Knit 1 rnd even.

YOKE

Work Rnds 1-14 of Chart 1 with Colors A and C, repeating to EOR. Cut Color A.

With Color C only, work Inc Rnd 3: *K3, M1; rep from * around. 168 (184, 192, 208, 216, 232) sts on needles. Knit 1 rnd even. Knit 1 rnd, inc 0 (2, 0, 2, 0, 2) sts evenly. 168 (186, 192, 210, 216, 234) sts on needles. Knit 1 rnd even.

Work Rnds 1-14 of Chart 2 with Colors A, B and C, repeating to EOR. Cut Colors A and B. With Color C only, knit 1 rnd, inc 0 (2, 0, 2, 0, 2) sts evenly. 168 (188, 192, 212, 216, 236) sts on needles. Knit 1 rnd even.

Work Inc Rnd 4: *K4, M1; rep from * around. 210 (235, 240, 265, 270, 295) sts on needles. Knit 1 rnd, dec 0 (1, 0, 1, 0, 1) st(s) at beg of rnd. 210 (234, 240, 264, 270, 294) sts on needles.

Work Rnds 1-14 of Chart 3 with Colors A, B and C, repeating to EOR. Cut Colors A and B. With Color C only, knit 1 (3, 4, 5, 6, 8) rnd(s).

BODY

Divide body and sleeves from yoke as follows:

With Color C only, *knit 64 (72, 74, 82, 84, 92) sts (front/back). Place next 41 (45, 46, 50, 51, 55) sts (sleeve) on circular stitch holder or waste yarn. Using Knitted cast-on method, CO 10 (10, 14, 14, 20, 20) sts for underarm. Rep from * once, then pm to indicate EOR. 148 (164, 176, 192, 208, 224) sts on needles.

Work in St st until body measures 5½" (5¾", 6½", 7½", 8", 8¼") [14 cm (14.5 cm, 16.5 cm, 19 cm, 20.5 cm, 21 cm)], or 6" [15 cm] less than desired length to hem.

Knit 1 rnd, dec 4 (2, 2, 0, 4, 2) sts evenly. 144 (162, 174, 192, 204, 222) sts on needles. Knit 1 rnd even.

Work Rnds 1-14 of Chart 4 with Colors A, B and C, repeating to EOR. Cut Colors A and B. With Color C only, knit 1 rnd, dec 0 (2, 2, 0, 0, 2) sts evenly. 144 (160, 172, 192, 204, 220) sts on needles. Knit 1 rnd even.

Switch to smaller needles and work 2x2 Ribbing for 6 rnds. Cut Color C. Join Color B and work 2x2 Ribbing for 3 rnds. Cut Color B. Join Color A and work 2x2 Ribbing for 2 rnds. BO all sts loosely using Icelandic bind-off method.

SLEEVES (MAKE 2)

With larger needles and using preferred needles for small-circumference knitting, beg at center of underarm with RS facing, join Color C and pick up and knit 5 (5, 7, 7, 10, 10) sts from CO sts at underarm, pick up and knit 1 st in gap between body and sleeve, knit 41 (45, 46, 50, 51, 55) sleeve sts from circular stitch holder or waste yarn, pick up and knit 1 st in gap between body and sleeve, then pick up and knit rem 5 (5, 7, 7, 10, 10) sts from underarm CO edge. 53 (57, 62, 66, 73, 77) sts on needles.

Join in the rnd and pm to indicate EOR, being careful not to twist sts. Knit 2 rnds even. Knit 1 rnd, dec 1 (1, 0, 0, 1, 1) st(s) at beg of rnd. 52 (56, 62, 66, 72, 76) sts on needles. Knit 1 rnd even.

Work Dec Rnd: K2, k2tog, knit to 4 sts before EOR marker, ssk, k2 (2 sts decreased).

Work in St st and rep Dec Rnd every 12th (9th, 9th, 7th, 5th, 4th) rnd, 4 (6, 6, 8, 11, 13) times. 42 (42, 48, 48, 48, 48) sts on needles.

Work in St st until sleeve measures 13¼" (13½", 13¾", 14", 14¼", 14½") [33.5 cm (34.5 cm, 35 cm, 35.5 cm, 36 cm, 37 cm)] or 5½" [14 cm] less than desired length to cuff.

Work Rnds 1-14 of Chart 4 with Colors A, B and C, repeating to EOR. Cut Colors A and B. With Color C only, knit 1 rnd, dec 2 (2, 4, 4, 0, 0) sts evenly. 40 (40, 44, 44, 48, 48) sts on needles. Knit 1 rnd even.

Switch to smaller needles and work 2x2 Ribbing for 6 rnds. Cut Color C. Join Color B and work 2x2 Ribbing for 3 rnds. Cut Color B. Join Color A and work 2x2 Ribbing for 2 rnds. BO all sts loosely using Icelandic bind-off method.

FINISHING

Weave in all loose ends with tapestry needle on the inside of the garment. Block to finished measurements.

Gimli
Men's Pullover
Chart 1: Yoke Chart A

Color Legend

- Knit with Color A: 1240 Dark Magenta
- Knit with Color C: 9967 Teal Heather

Dominant Color

Background Color

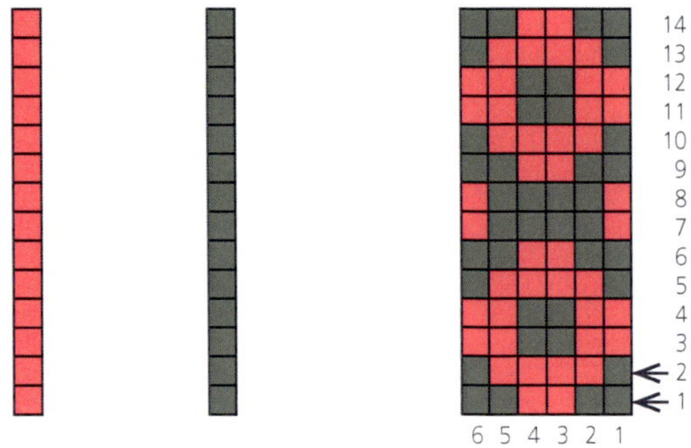

Gimli
Men's Pullover
Chart 2: Yoke Chart B

Color Legend

- Knit with Color A: 1240 Dark Magenta
- Knit with Color B: 0051 White
- Knit with Color C: 9967 Teal Heather

Dominant Color

Background Color

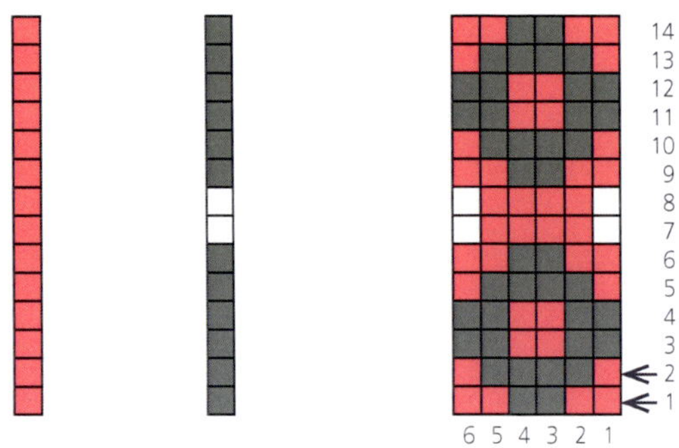

Gimli
Men's Pullover
Chart 3: Yoke Chart C

Color Legend

- Knit with Color A: 1240 Dark Magenta
- Knit with Color B: 0051 White
- Knit with Color C: 9967 Teal Heather

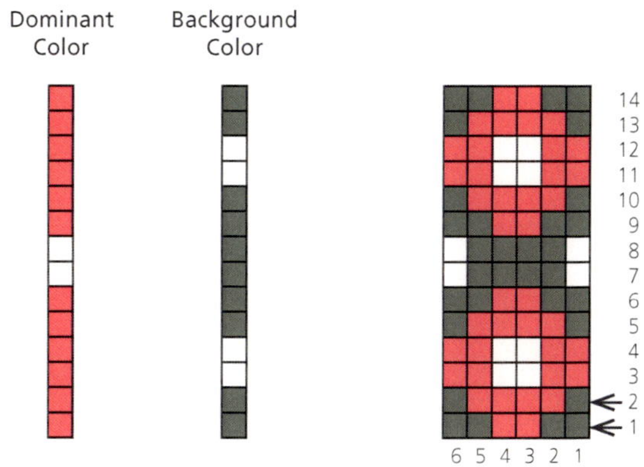

Gimli
Men's Pullover
Chart 4: Band Chart

Color Legend

- Knit with Color A: 1240 Dark Magenta
- Knit with Color B: 0051 White
- Knit with Color C: 9967 Teal Heather

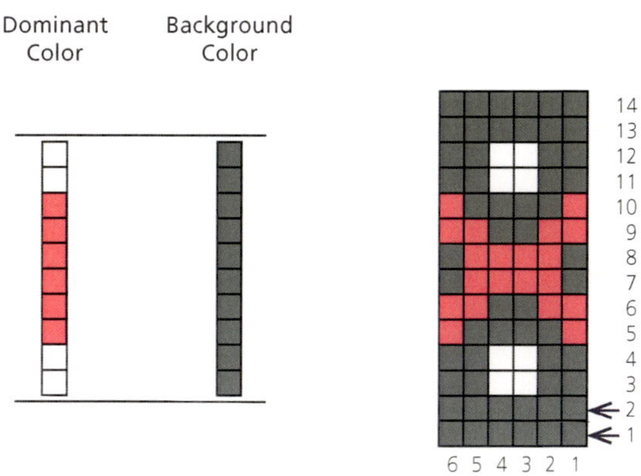

Gimli
Men's Pullover
Schematic

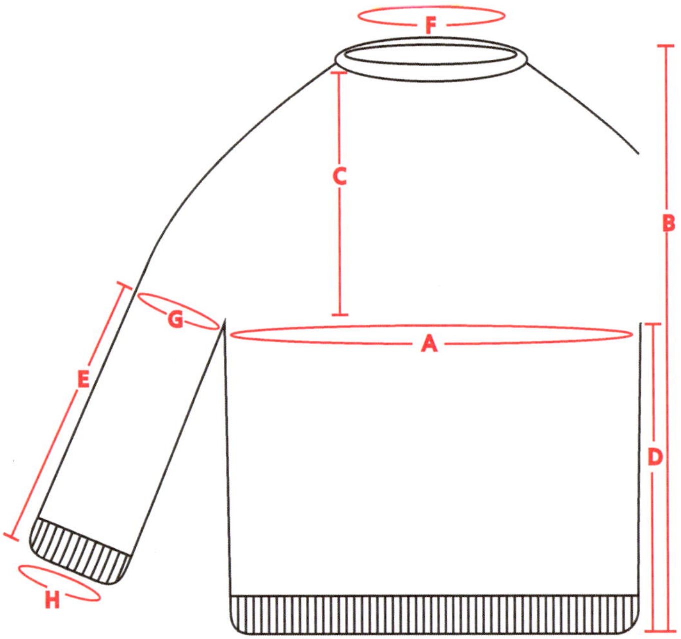

A CHEST CIRCUMFERENCE:
39½ (43¾, 47, 51¼, 55½, 59¾) inches
98.5 (109.5, 117.5, 128, 138.5, 149.5) cm

B PULLOVER LENGTH:
27¾ (28¼, 29¼, 30½, 31¼, 31¾) inches
69.5 (71, 73.5, 76.5, 78.5, 80) cm

C YOKE DEPTH:
13¾ (14¼, 14½, 14½, 14¾, 15¼) inches
34.5 (35.5, 36, 36.5, 37, 38) cm

D BODY LENGTH:
11½ (11¾, 12½, 13½, 14, 14¼) inches
29 (29.5, 31.5, 34, 35.5, 36) cm

E SLEEVE LENGTH:
18¾ (19, 19¼, 19½, 19¾, 20) inches
47.5 (48.5, 49, 49.5, 50, 51) cm

F NECK CIRCUMFERENCE:
15 (16, 17, 18¼, 19¼, 20¼) inches
37.5 (40, 42.5, 45.5, 48, 50.5) cm

G UPPER ARM CIRCUMFERENCE:
14¼ (15¼, 16½, 17½, 19½, 20½) inches
35.5 (38, 41.5, 44, 48.5, 51.5) cm

H CUFF CIRCUMFERENCE:
10¾ (10¾, 11¾, 11¾, 12¾, 12¾) inches
26.5 (26.5, 29.5, 29.5, 32, 32) cm

Hildur

Hildur pays tribute to the Queen of the Elves or *Huldufólk*, hidden people who are thought to exist alongside the Icelanders. Even today, many inhabitants continue to believe in their existence, often building tiny houses for them in their gardens and even miniature churches in an attempt to convert them to Christianity. Road construction projects have also been halted recently in order to study their effects on the elves and the rocks in which they are purported to live. Even if some people don't believe in them, it's better to be safe than sorry, just in case.

I wanted to design a delicate gray pullover that would feature brightly colored horizontal bands inspired by Fair Isle traditions. I also wanted to include gentle waist shaping in order to create a petite silhouette that would be fitting for an elfish queen. Corrugated ribbing and a rolled neckband finish off a design that looks very polished, but is relaxed and comfortable at the same time.

Project Overview

SIZES

XS (S, M, L, XL, XXL) to fit bust circumference of 34" (38", 42", 46", 50", 54") [86.5 cm (96.5 cm, 106.5 cm, 117 cm, 127 cm, 137 cm)] with 2¼-3" [3.5-5.5 cm] of positive ease intended.

Shown in Size XS with 2¼" [4 cm] of positive ease.

FINISHED MEASUREMENTS

Bust Circumference: 36¼" (40½", 44¾", 49", 52¼", 56½") [90.5 cm (101.5 cm, 112 cm, 122.5 cm, 130.5 cm, 141.5 cm)].

Pullover Length: 22¼" (23", 23½", 24½", 25¼", 26") [55.5 cm (57.5 cm, 59 cm, 61.5 cm, 63 cm, 65 cm)].

YARN

Ístex Álafosslopi: 100% Icelandic wool; 109 yds [100 m] per 3.5 oz [100 g] skein.

- Color A: 0056 Light Ash Heather; 5 (6, 7, 8, 9, 10) skeins.
- Color B: 9964 Golden Heather; 1 skein for all sizes.
- Color C: 9966 Cypress Green Heather; 1 skein for all sizes.
- Color D: 1240 Dark Magenta; 1 skein for all sizes.
- Color E: 0159 Orchid; 1 skein for all sizes.
- Color F: 9965 Chartreuse Green Heather; 1 skein for all sizes.
- Color G: 9958 Light Indigo; 1 skein for all sizes.

NEEDLES

US #9 [5.5 mm], or size needed to obtain gauge;

- All sizes: 24" [60 cm], 32" [80 cm], and 40" [100 cm] circular needles.
- Sizes XL-XXL: 60" [150 cm] circular needles.

- Optional: double-pointed needles for small-circumference knitting.

Note: Begin with the shortest circular needles and switch to longer lengths as needed while working the yoke. Use your preferred method of small-circumference knitting to work the neckband and the sleeves.

NOTIONS

3 stitch markers (including one to indicate end of round).

3 short circular stitch holders or waste yarn (to hold live stitches for neckband and sleeves).

Blunt tapestry needle.
Blocking pins, if desired.

GAUGE

15 sts and 20 rnds = 4" [10 cm] in St st, after blocking.

Construction Notes

This garment is worked seamlessly in the round from the top down.

Directions for the Provisional Cast On, the Knitted Cast On and the Icelandic Bind Off, as well as other useful information, can be found in the Special Techniques section of the book.

The yoke is knit in the round with increases occurring immediately after the cast on, as well as before and after each band of stranded colorwork.

The yoke is then divided to work the body, with additional stitches cast on at the underarms, while the sleeve stitches are held separately.

The sleeves are worked from the upper arm down with stitches picked up from the cast-on edge at the underarms and are tapered with decreases to the cuff.

The neckband is worked in stockinette from held stitches to produce a rolled edge at the neck.

Corrugated ribbing is worked at the hem and the cuffs.

Pattern Instructions

YOKE

Using Provisional cast-on method, CO 56 (60, 64, 68, 72, 76) sts using Color A. Knit 1 row. Join in the rnd and pm to indicate EOR, being careful not to twist sts.

Work Inc Rnd 1: *K2, M1; rep from * around. 84 (90, 96, 102, 108, 114) sts on needles. Knit 2 (3, 4, 4, 5, 6) rnds.

Work Inc Rnd 2: *K2, M1; rep from * around. 126 (135, 144, 153, 162, 171) sts on needles. Knit 1 rnd even. Cut Color A. With Color B only, knit 1 rnd, inc 0 (5, 10, 15, 20, 25) sts evenly. 126 (140, 154, 168, 182, 196) sts on needles.

Work Rnds 1-7 of Chart 1 with Colors B, C and D, repeating to EOR. With Color B only, knit 1 rnd, inc 0 (4, 8, 12, 16, 20) sts evenly. 126 (144, 162, 180, 198, 216) sts on needles.

With Color E only, work Inc Rnd 3: *K3, M1; rep from * around. 168 (192, 216, 240, 264, 288) sts on needles.

Work Rnds 1-13 of Chart 2 with Colors B, C, D, E, F and G, repeating to EOR. Cut Colors F and G.

With Color E only, work Inc Rnd 4: *K12, M1; rep from * around. 182 (208, 234, 260, 286, 312) sts. Cut Color E. With Color B only, knit 1 rnd, inc 14 (16, 18, 6, 8, 10) sts evenly. 196 (224, 252, 266, 294, 322) sts on needles.

Work Rnds 1-7 of Chart 1 with Colors B, C and D, repeating to EOR. Cut Colors C and D. With Color B only, knit 1 rnd, dec 0 (4, 12, 2, 10, 14) sts evenly. 196 (220, 240, 264, 284, 308) sts on needles. Cut Color B. With Color A only, knit 2 (3, 3, 4, 4, 5) rnds even.

BODY

Divide body and sleeves from yoke as follows:

With Color A only, *knit 60 (68, 74, 82, 86, 94) sts (front/back). Place next 38 (42, 46, 50, 56, 60) sts (sleeve) on circular stitch holder or waste yarn. Using Knitted cast-on method, CO 4 (4, 5, 5, 6, 6) sts for underarm, pm, then CO 4 (4, 5, 5, 6, 6) more underarm sts. Rep from * once, then pm to indicate EOR. 68 (76, 84, 92, 98, 106) sts each for front and back; 136 (152, 168, 184, 196, 212) sts on needles.

Note: The 2 new markers divide the body into the front and the back of the garment.

Knit 4 rnds.

Work Dec Rnd: *K6, k2tog, k to 8 sts before next marker, ssk, k6, sl m; rep from * once (4 sts decreased).

Work in St st and rep Dec Rnd every 4th (4th, 4th, 5th, 5th, 6th) rnd 3 times. 120 (136, 152, 168, 180, 196) sts on needles. Knit 8 rnds.

Work Inc Rnd: *K6, M1R, k to 6 sts before next marker, M1L, k6, sl m; rep from * once (4 sts increased).

Work in St st and rep Inc Rnd every 4th (4th, 4th, 5th, 5th, 6th) rnd 3 (3, 3, 2, 3, 2) times. 136 (152, 168, 180, 196, 208) sts on needles. Knit 1 (3, 5, 8, 5, 7) rnd(s).

Cut Color A. With Color B only, knit 1 rnd, inc 4 (2, 0, 2, 0, 2) sts evenly. 140 (154, 168, 182, 196, 210) sts on needles.

Work Rnds 1-17 of Chart 1 with Colors B, C and D, repeating to EOR. Cut Colors C and D. With Color B only, knit 1 rnd, dec 0 (2, 0, 2, 0, 2) sts evenly. 140 (152, 168, 180, 196, 208) sts on needles. Cut Color B. With Color A only, knit 4 rnds even.

Work Rnds 1-8 of Chart 3 with Colors A, E, F and G, repeating to EOR. Cut Colors E, F and G. With Color A only, knit 1 rnd. BO all sts loosely using Icelandic bind-off method.

SLEEVES (MAKE 2)

Using preferred needles for small-circumference knitting, beg at center of underarm with RS facing, join Color A and pick up and knit 4 (4, 5, 5, 6, 6) sts from CO sts at underarm, pick up and knit 1 st in gap between body and sleeve, knit 38 (42, 46, 50, 56, 60) sleeves sts from circular stitch holder or waste yarn, pick up and knit 1 st between body and sleeve, then pick up and knit rem 4 (4, 5, 5, 6, 6) sts from underarm CO edge. 48 (52, 58, 62, 70, 74) sts on needles.

Join in the rnd and pm to indicate EOR, being careful not to twist sts. Knit 4 rnds.

Work Dec Rnd: K2, k2tog, knit to 4 sts before EOR marker, ssk, k2 (2 sts decreased).

Work in St st and rep Dec Rnd every 18th (11th, 7th, 6th, 4th, 4th) rnd, 2 (4, 7, 9, 13, 15) times. 42 sts on needles.

Work in St st until sleeve measures 12" (12½", 13¼", 13½", 14", 14½") [30 cm (31 cm, 33 cm, 34 cm, 35 cm, 36 cm)], or 4½" [11 cm] less than desired length. Cut Color A. With Color B only, knit 1 rnd.

Work Rnds 1-7 of Chart 1 with Colors B, C and D, repeating to EOR. Cut Colors C and D. With Color B only, knit 1 rnd, inc 0 (0, 0, 0, 2, 2) sts evenly. 42 (42, 42, 42, 44, 44) sts on needles. Cut Color B. With Color A only, knit 1 rnd even. Knit 1 rnd, dec 6 (6, 2, 2, 0, 0) sts evenly. 36 (36, 40, 40, 44, 44) sts on needles. Knit 2 rnds even.

Work Rnds 1-8 of Chart 3 with Colors A, E, F and G, repeating to EOR. Cut Colors E, F and G. With Color A only, knit 1 rnd. BO all sts loosely using Icelandic bind-off method.

NECKBAND

Using preferred needles for small-circumference knitting and with RS facing, join Color A and knit 56 (60, 64, 68, 72, 76) neckband sts from circular stitch holder or waste yarn. Join in the rnd and pm to indicate EOR.

Knit 10 rnds. BO all sts loosely using Icelandic bind-off method.

FINISHING

Weave in all loose ends with tapestry needle on the inside of the garment. Block to finished measurements.

Hildur
Women's Pullover
Chart 1: Yoke Chart A

Color
Legend

- Knit with Color B: 9964 Golden Heather
- Knit with Color C: 9966 Cypress Green Heather
- Knit with Color D: 1240 Dark Magenta

Dominant Color

Background Color

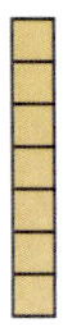

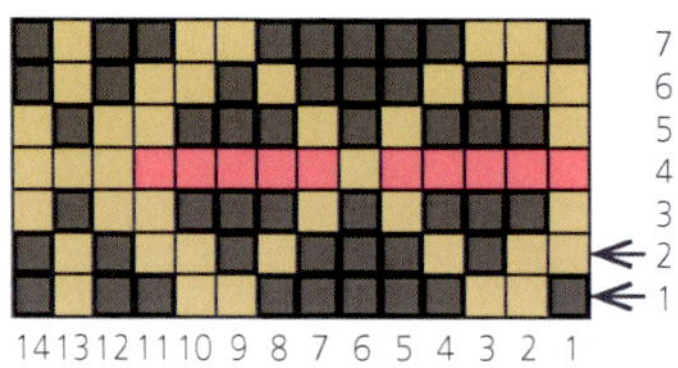

Hildur
Women's Pullover
Chart 2: Yoke Chart B

Color Legend

- Knit with Color B: 9964 Golden Heather
- Knit with Color C: 9966 Cypress Green Heather
- Knit with Color D: 1240 Dark Magenta
- Knit with Color E: 0159 Orchid
- Knit with Color F: 9965 Chartreuse Green Heather
- Knit with Color G: 9958 Light Indigo

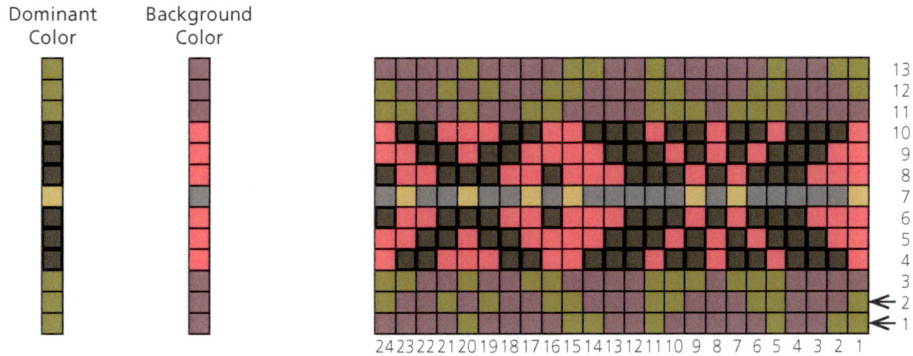

Hildur
Women's Pullover
Chart 3: Ribbing Chart

Color Legend

- Knit with Color A: 0056 Light Ash Heather
- Purl with Color A: 0056 Light Ash Heather
- Purl with Color E: 0159 Orchid
- Purl with Color F: 9965 Chartreuse Green Heather
- Purl with Color G: 9958 Light Indigo

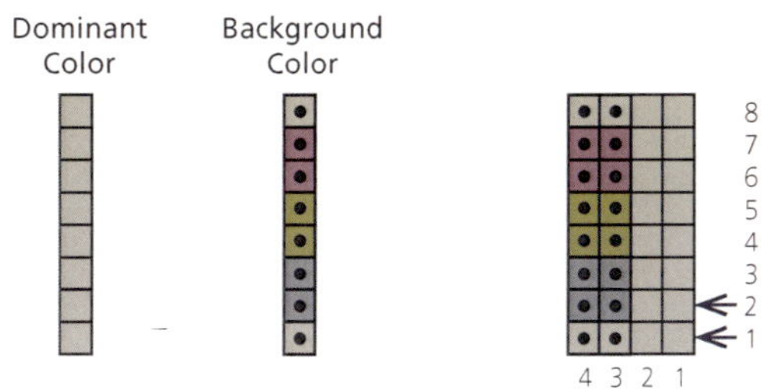

Hildur
Women's Pullover
Schematic

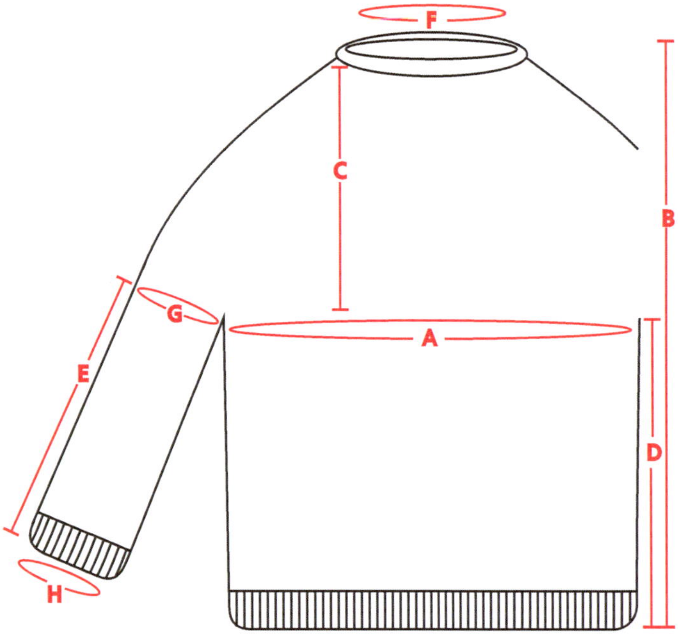

A BUST CIRCUMFERENCE:
36¼ (40½, 44¾, 49, 52¼, 56½) inches
90.5 (101.5, 112, 122.5, 130.5, 141.5) cm

B PULLOVER LENGTH:
22¼ (23, 23½, 24½, 25¼, 26) inches
55.5 (57.5, 59, 61.5, 63, 65) cm

C YOKE DEPTH:
8¼ (8½, 8¾, 9, 9¼, 9½) inches
20.5 (21.5, 22, 22.5, 23, 24) cm

D BODY LENGTH:
12¼ (12½, 13, 13¾, 14¼, 14½) inches
30.5 (31.5, 32.5, 34.5, 35.5, 36.5) cm

E SLEEVE LENGTH:
16½ (17, 17¾, 18, 18½, 19) inches
41 (42, 44, 45, 46, 47) cm

F NECK CIRCUMFERENCE:
15 (16, 17, 18¼, 19¼, 20¼) inches
37.5 (40, 42.5, 45.5, 48, 50.5) cm

G UPPER ARM CIRCUMFERENCE:
12¾ (13¾, 15½, 16½, 18¾, 19¾) inches
32 (34.5, 38.5, 41.5, 46.5, 49.5) cm

H CUFF CIRCUMFERENCE:
9½ (9½, 10¾, 10¾, 11¾, 11¾) inches
24 (24, 26.5, 26.5, 29.5, 29.5) cm

Rúntur

Rúntur is the word for the infamous bar crawl that takes place in Reykjavík on weekends. In small towns all over Iceland, young people drive their cars slowly around the same circuitous route in order to visit with their friends. This tradition, like many of these inhabitants, moved to the nation's capital and developed into something new.

The concept behind this pullover is that you started it at the beginning of the night, when you were sober. You still had the ability to focus on such details as corrugated ribbing and offset pattern repeats. As you made your way from stop to stop on the bar crawl, however, you became progressively tipsy. When it came time to connect the body and sleeves to form the yoke, you were completely drunk and you put everything together inside out. You used the wrong background color on the pattern repeat at the beginning of the yoke. By the time the sun rose the next morning as you finished the yoke, you had given up on any attempts at corrugated ribbing at the neck.

Project Overview

SIZES

XS (S, M, L, XL, XXL) to fit bust circumference of 34" (38", 42", 46", 50", 54") [86.5 cm (96.5 cm, 106.5 cm, 117 cm, 127 cm, 137 cm)] with 4½-5¾" [9.5-12.5 cm] of positive ease intended.

Shown in Size S with 4¾" [10 cm] of positive ease.

FINISHED MEASUREMENTS

Bust Circumference: 38½" (42¾", 47", 51¼", 55½", 59¾") [96 cm (106.5 cm, 117.5 cm, 128 cm, 139 cm, 149.5 cm)].

Pullover Length: 24½" (24¾", 25¾", 26", 26¾", 27") [62 cm (62.5 cm, 65 cm, 65.5 cm, 67.5 cm, 68 cm)].

YARN

Ístex Álafosslopi: 100% Icelandic wool; 109 yds [100 m] per 3.5 oz [100 g] skein.

- Color A: 1232 Arctic Exposure; 5 (6, 7, 8, 9, 10) skeins.
- Color B: 0118 Navy; 1 (1, 1, 2, 2, 2) skein(s).
- Color C: 9958 Light Indigo; 1 skein for all sizes.
- Color D: 1239 Winter Morning; 1 skein for all sizes.
- Color E: 0008 Light Denim Heather; 1 skein for all sizes.

NEEDLES

US #10 [6.0 mm], or size needed to obtain gauge;

- All sizes: 24" [60 cm] and 32" [80 cm] circular needles.
- Sizes M-XXL: 40" [100 cm] circular needles.
- Sizes XL-XXL: 60" [150 cm] circular needles.
- Optional: double-pointed needles for small-circumference knitting.

US #8 [5.0 mm], or two sizes smaller than gauge needles;

- All sizes: 24" [60 cm] and 32" [80 cm] circular needles.
- Optional: double-pointed needles for small-circumference knitting.

Note: Work the body with the needle length closest to the finished bust measurement. Use the longest needles indicated for your size when joining the body and the sleeves together at the beginning of the yoke. Switch to shorter lengths as needed while working the yoke. Use your preferred method of small-circumference knitting to work the neckband and the sleeves.

NOTIONS

1 stitch marker (to indicate end of round).

4 stitch holders or waste yarn (to hold stitches at each underarm).

1 long and 2 short circular stitch holders or waste yarn (to hold live stitches for body and sleeves).

Blunt tapestry needle.
Blocking pins, if desired.

GAUGE

15 sts and 20 rnds = 4" [10 cm] in St st using larger needles, after blocking.

Construction Notes

This garment is worked seamlessly in the round from the bottom up.

Directions for the Knitted Cast On, the Icelandic Bind Off and the Kitchener Stitch, as well as other useful information, can be found in the Special Techniques section of the book.

The body is worked from the hem to the underarms in stockinette with stranded colorwork without shaping.

The sleeves are worked similarly from the cuff to the underarm and are shaped with paired, symmetrical increases.

The stitches for the body and both sleeves are joined together inside out on one set of circular needles to work the yoke.

The yoke is worked in stockinette on the wrong side. Once turned right side out, the reverse stockinette and stranded floats will be intentionally exposed.

The underarm stitches are placed on stitch holders or waste yarn and are grafted together during the finishing process.

Corrugated ribbing is worked at the hem and the cuffs, while 2x2 Ribbing is worked at the neckband.

Ribbing is always worked using the smaller needles.

Stitch Patterns

2X2 RIBBING

Worked over a multiple of 4 sts; 1-rnd repeat.
Rnd 1: *K2, p2; rep from * around.
Rep Rnd 1 as directed.

Pattern Instructions

BODY

With smaller needles and using Knitted cast-on method, CO 136 (152, 164, 180, 196, 212) sts using Color A. Join in the rnd and pm to indicate EOR, being careful not to twist sts. Knit 1 rnd.

Work Rnds 1-8 of Chart 1 with Colors A, B, C and D, repeating to EOR. Cut Colors B, C and D. With Color A only, knit 1 rnd.

Switch to larger needles and knit 1 rnd even. Knit 1 rnd, inc 8 (8, 12, 12, 12, 12) sts evenly. 144 (160, 176, 192, 208, 224) sts on needles. Knit 2 rnds even.

Work Rnds 1-8 of Chart 2 with Colors A, B and C, repeating to EOR. Cut Colors B and C. With Color A only, knit 8 rnds.

Work Rnds 1-8 of Chart 3 with Colors A, B and C, repeating to EOR. Cut Colors B and C.

With Color A only, work in St st until body measures 14" (14", 14¾", 14¾", 15¼", 15¼") [35.5 cm (35.5 cm, 37.5 cm, 37.5 cm, 38.5 cm, 38.5 cm)], or desired length to underarm.

Knit to 7 (8, 9, 10, 11, 12) sts before EOR marker. Place the next 14 (16, 18, 20, 22, 24) sts on stitch holder or waste yarn, removing marker. Place the rem 130 (144, 158, 172, 186, 200) sts on long circular stitch holder or waste yarn and set aside.

SLEEVES (MAKE 2)

With smaller needles, using preferred needles for small-circumference knitting and using Knitted cast-on method, CO 40 (40, 40, 44, 44, 44) sts using Color A. Join in the rnd and pm to indicate EOR, being careful not to twist sts. Knit 1 rnd.

Work Rnds 1-8 of Chart 1 with Colors A, B, C and D, repeating to EOR. Cut Colors B, C and D. With Color A only, knit 1 rnd.

Switch to larger needles and knit 1 rnd even. Knit 1 rnd, inc 8 (8, 8, 4, 4, 4) sts evenly. 48 sts on needles. Knit 2 rnds even.

Work Rnds 1-8 of Chart 2 with Colors A, B and C, repeating to EOR. Cut Colors B and C. With Color A only, knit 8 rnds.

Work Rnds 1-8 of Chart 3 with Colors A, B and C, repeating to EOR. Cut Colors B and C.

With Color A only, work in St st and inc 1 st at beg and end of every 23rd (12th, 8th, 6th, 4th, 3rd) rnd, 2 (4, 6, 8, 11, 14) times. 52 (56, 60, 64, 70, 76) sts on needles.

Work in St st until sleeve measures 17½" (18", 18", 18¾", 20½", 20¾") [44.5 cm (45.5 cm, 45.5 cm, 47.5 cm, 52 cm, 52.5 cm)], or desired length to underarm.

Knit to 7 (8, 9, 10, 11, 12) sts before EOR marker. Place the next 14 (16, 18, 20, 22, 24) sts on stitch holder or waste yarn, removing marker. Place the rem 38 (40, 42, 44, 48, 52) sts on short circular stitch holder or waste yarn and set aside.

YOKE

Turn body and sleeves inside out. With the longest larger needles, WS facing and using Color A, join body and sleeves together as follows:

Knit 38 (40, 42, 44, 48, 52) sts of first sleeve, knit 65 (72, 79, 86, 93, 100) sts of body for front. Place next 14 (16, 18, 20, 22, 24) sts of body on stitch holder or waste yarn. Knit 38 (40, 42, 44, 48, 52) sts of second sleeve, knit rem 65 (72, 79, 86, 93, 100) sts of body for back, pm to indicate EOR. 206 (224, 242, 260, 282, 304) sts on needles.

Size XS only:

Knit 1 rnd, inc 2 sts evenly. 208 sts on needles.

All other sizes:

Knit 1 rnd, dec - (0, 2, 4, 10, 0) sts evenly. - (224, 240, 256, 272, 304) sts on needles.

All sizes:

Work Rnds 1-8 of Chart 4 with Colors A, B and E, repeating to EOR. Cut Colors B and E. With Color A only, knit 2 rnds.

Work Dec Rnd 1: *K6, k2tog; rep from * around. 182 (196, 210, 224, 238, 266) sts on needles. Knit 2 rnds.

Size XL only:

Knit 1 rnd, inc 2 sts evenly. 240 sts on needles.

All other sizes:

Knit 1 rnd, dec 6 (4, 2, 0, -, 10) sts evenly. 176 (192, 208, 224, - , 256) sts on needles.

All sizes:

Knit 2 rnds even.

Work Rnds 1-8 of Chart 5 with Colors A, B and E, repeating to EOR. Cut Colors B and E. With Color A only, knit 1 rnd, dec 1 (3, 5, 0, 2, 4) st(s) evenly. 175 (189, 203, 224, 238, 252) sts on needles. Knit 1 rnd even.

Work Dec Rnd 2: *K5, k2tog; rep from * around. 150 (162, 174, 192, 204, 216) sts on needles. Knit 1 rnd even. Knit 1 rnd, dec 6 (2, 6, 0, 4, 0) sts evenly. 144 (160, 168, 192, 200, 216) sts on needles. Knit 1 rnd even.

Work Chart 6 with Colors A, D and E, repeating to EOR, skipping rnds where indicated. Cut Colors D and E.

With Color A only, work Dec Rnd 3: *K2, k2tog; rep from * around. 108 (120, 126, 144, 150, 162) sts on needles. Knit 1 rnd even. Knit 1 rnd, dec 4 (8, 6, 8, 6, 10) sts evenly. 104 (112, 120, 136, 144, 152) on needles. Knit 1 rnd even.

Work Rnds 1-10 of Chart 7 with Colors A, B and D, repeating to EOR, decreasing sts where indicated. 78 (84, 90, 102, 108, 114) sts on needles. Cut Colors B and D.

With Color A only, knit 1 rnd, dec 18 (16, 18, 26, 28, 30) evenly. 60 (68, 72, 76, 80, 84) sts on needles.

NECKBAND

Switch to smaller needles and knit 1 rnd. Work 2x2 Ribbing for 8 rnds. BO all sts loosely using Icelandic bind-off method.

FINISHING

Graft underarm sts together using Kitchener Stitch method. Weave in all loose ends with tapestry needle on the inside of the garment. Block to finished measurements.

Rúntur Women's Pullover Chart 1: Ribbing Chart

Color Legend

- Knit with Color A: 1232 Arctic Exposure
- Purl with Color A: 1232 Arctic Exposure
- Purl with Color B: 0118 Navy
- Purl with Color C: 9958 Light Indigo
- Purl with Color D: 1239 Winter Morning

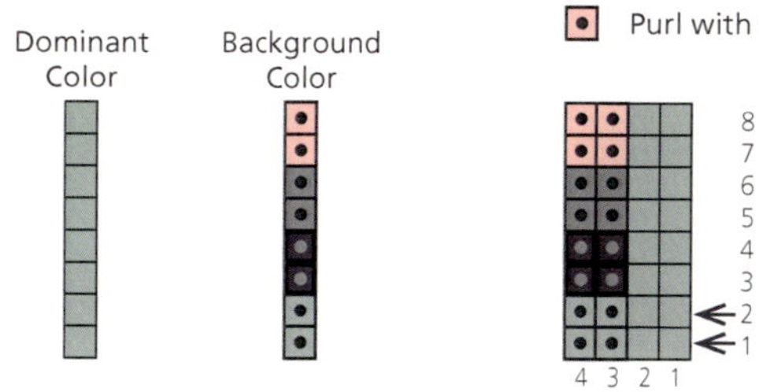

Rúntur Women's Pullover Chart 2: Band Chart A

Color Legend

- Knit with Color A: 1232 Arctic Exposure
- Knit with Color B: 0118 Navy
- Knit with Color C: 9958 Light Indigo

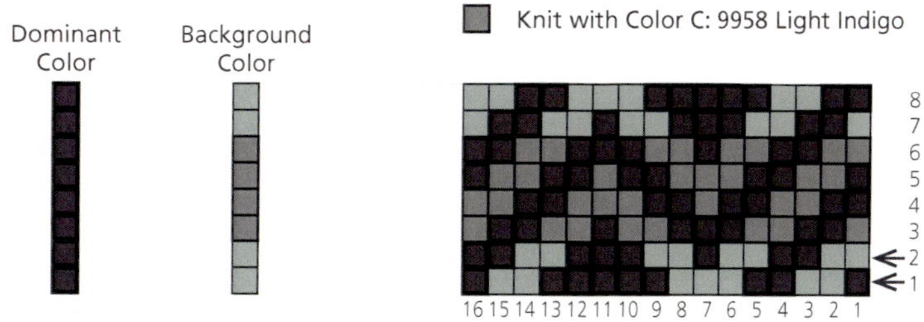

Rúntur Women's Pullover Chart 3: Band Chart B

Color Legend

- Knit with Color A: 1232 Arctic Exposure
- Knit with Color B: 0118 Navy
- Knit with Color C: 9958 Light Indigo

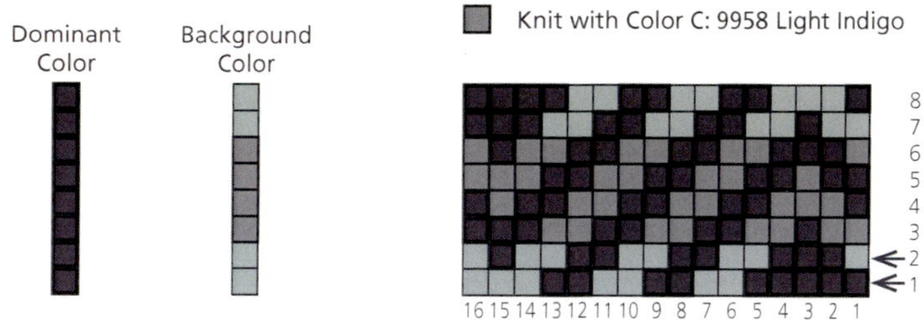

Rúntur Women's Pullover Chart 4: Yoke Chart A

Color Legend

- Knit with Color A: 1232 Arctic Exposure
- Knit with Color B: 0118 Navy
- Knit with Color E: 0008 Light Denim Heather

Dominant Color | Background Color

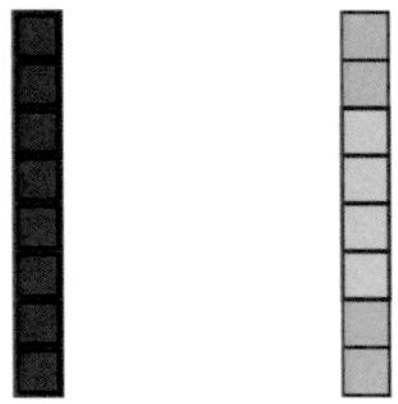

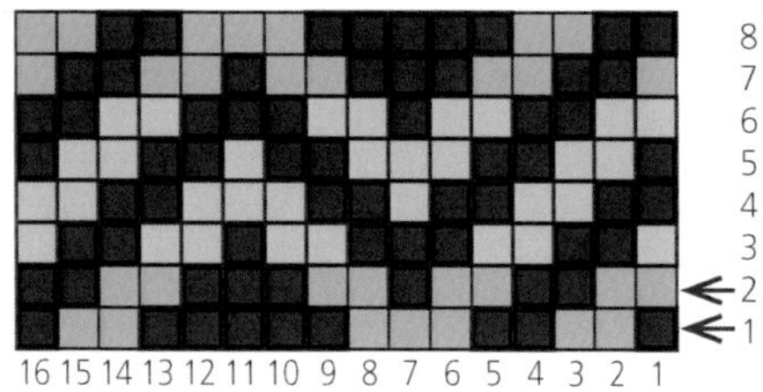

Rúntur Women's Pullover Chart 5: Yoke Chart B

Color Legend

- Knit with Color A: 1232 Arctic Exposure
- Knit with Color B: 0118 Navy
- Knit with Color E: 0008 Light Denim Heather

Dominant Color | Background Color

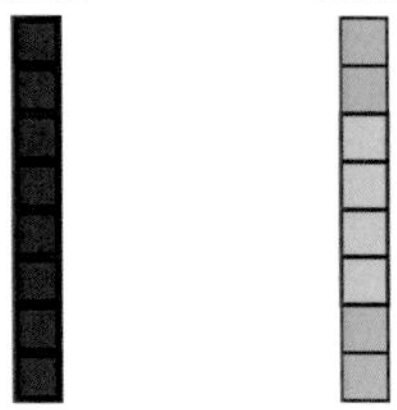

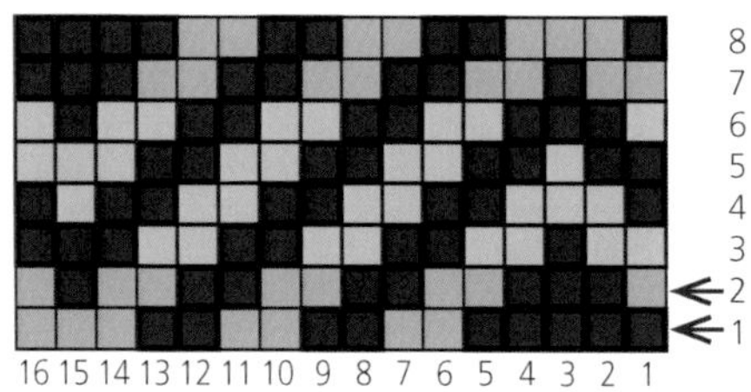

Rúntur
Women's Pullover
Chart 6: Yoke Chart C

Color Legend

- Knit with Color A: 1232 Arctic Exposure
- Knit with Color D: 1239 Winter Morning
- Knit with Color E: 0008 Light Denim Heather

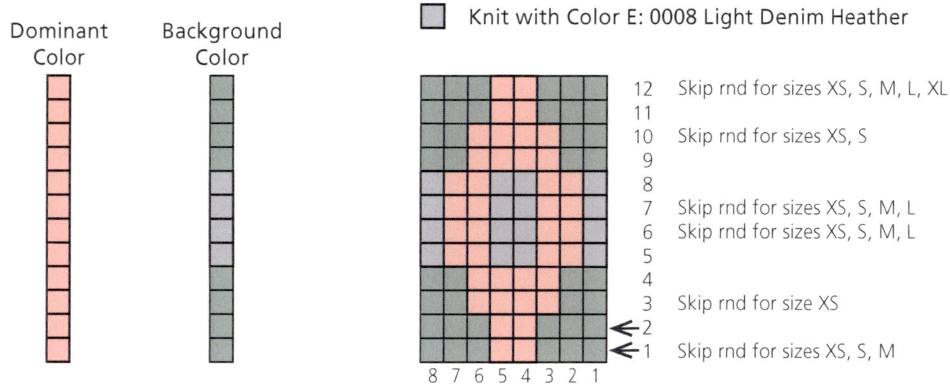

Rúntur
Women's Pullover
Chart 7: Yoke Chart D

Color Legend

- Knit with Color A: 1232 Arctic Exposure
- Knit with Color B: 0118 Navy
- Knit with Color D: 1239 Winter Morning

Stitch Legend

- No Stitch
- K2tog with Color Indicated

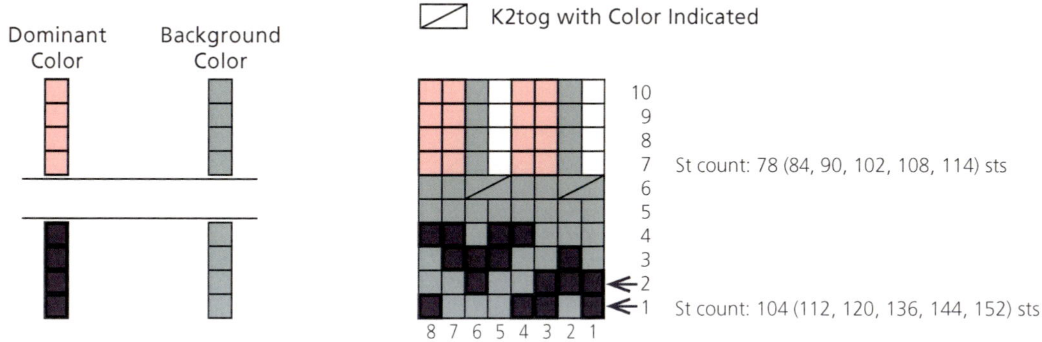

Rúntur
Women's Pullover
Schematic

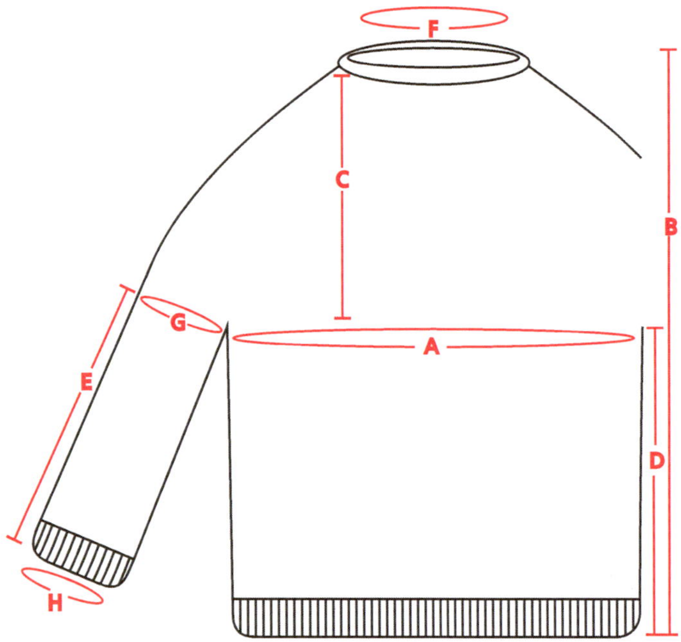

A BUST CIRCUMFERENCE:
38½ (42¾, 47, 51¼, 55½, 59¾) inches
96 (106.5, 117.5, 128, 139, 149.5) cm

B PULLOVER LENGTH:
24½ (24¾, 25¾, 26, 26¾, 27) inches
62 (62.5, 65, 65.5, 67.5, 68) cm

C YOKE DEPTH:
10½ (10¾, 11, 11¼, 11½, 11¾) inches
26.5 (27, 27.5, 28, 29, 29.5) cm

D BODY LENGTH:
14 (14, 14¾, 14¾, 15¼, 15¼) inches
35.5 (35.5, 37.5, 37.5, 38.5, 38.5) cm

E SLEEVE LENGTH:
17½ (18, 18, 18¾, 20½, 20¾) inches
44.5 (45.5, 45.5, 47.5, 52, 52.5) cm

F NECK CIRCUMFERENCE:
16 (18¼, 19¼, 20¼, 21¼, 22½) inches
40 (45.5, 48, 50.5, 53.5, 56) cm

G UPPER ARM CIRCUMFERENCE:
13¾ (15, 16, 17, 18¾, 20¼) inches
34.5 (37.5, 40, 42.5, 46.5, 50.5) cm

H CUFF CIRCUMFERENCE:
10¾ (10¾, 10¾, 11¾, 11¾, 11¾) inches
26.5 (26.5, 26.5, 29.5, 29.5, 29.5) cm

Katla

Katla is one of the many volcanos that dot the Icelandic geography. It is also a lot easier to pronounce than many of the other volcanos I could have chosen, such as Bárðarbunga and Eyjafjallajökull, to name this pullover. I had always imagined that Iceland was nothing but spectacular fjords and waterfalls, snow-topped glaciers and fields of green. Instead, I was confronted by a lunar landscape full of jagged rocks and volcanic lava fields. When I traveled by bus from Keflavík, the main airport in Iceland, to Reykjavík, I was surprised to see just how otherworldly the countryside really was.

I had always wanted to design an Aran-type sweater out of Lopi using only a single color, even though most Icelandic pullovers are worked with multicolored, seamless yokes. After all, there is no reason why one couldn't create a complicated, pieced design with cables everywhere. When it came to grading the garment, I decided to rearrange the placement of the cables to fit my desired stitch counts. To me, these undulating stitches suggest the rise of both smoke and steam from the volcanos that produced this island nation.

Project Overview

SIZES

S (M, L, XL) to fit bust circumference of 34" (40", 46", 52") [86.5 cm (101.5 cm, 117 cm, 132 cm)] with 2" [3-3.5 cm] of positive ease intended.

Shown in Size M with 2" [3.5 cm] of positive ease in 9958 Light Indigo.

Shown in Size XL with 2" [3 cm] of positive ease in 9969 Fuchsia Heather.

FINISHED MEASUREMENTS

Bust Circumference: 36" (42", 48", 54") [90 cm (106 cm, 120 cm, 136 cm].

Pullover Length: 21¾" (24¼", 26", 27½") [55 cm (61 cm, 66 cm, 70 cm)].

YARN

Ístex Álafosslopi: 100% Icelandic wool; 109 yds [100 m] per 3.5 oz [100 g] skein. Any color; 7 (8, 9, 10) skeins.

NEEDLES

US #10 [6.0 mm], or size needed to obtain gauge;

- Straight or circular needles for working flat.

US #8 [5.0 mm], or two sizes smaller than gauge needles;

- Straight or circular needles for working flat.
- 16" [40 cm] circular needles for neckband.

NOTIONS

1 stitch marker (to indicate end of round).

2 stitch holders or waste yarn (to hold live stitches at each saddle strap).

Blunt tapestry needle.
Blocking pins, if desired.

GAUGE

16 sts and 20 rnds = 4" [10 cm] in St st using larger needles, after blocking.

Construction Notes

This garment is worked in pieces from the bottom up.

Directions for the Channel Island Cast On and the Icelandic Bind Off, as well as other useful information, can be found in the Special Techniques section of the book.

The back and front are worked flat from the hem to the shoulders with armhole shaping and front neck shaping.

The sleeves are worked flat from the cuff to the underarm and are shaped with paired, symmetrical increases, followed by sleeve cap shaping and saddle straps.

The stitches for the saddle straps are placed on stitch holders or waste yarn and are joined with stitches picked up from the back and the front for the neckband.

1x1 Ribbing is always worked using the smaller needles.

Stitch Legend

C2BW: Cross 2 Back on WS (sl 1 on cn, cnb, p1, p1 from cn).

C2F: Cross 2 Front (sl 1 on cn, cnf, k1, k1 from cn).

C4B: Cross 4 Back (sl 2 on cn, cnb, k2, k2 from cn).

C4F: Cross 4 Front (sl 2 on cn, cnf, k2, k2 from cn).

C8B: Cross 8 Back (sl 4 on cn, cnb, k4, k4 from cn).

C8F: Cross 8 Front (sl 4 on cn, cnf, k4, k4 from cn).

T3B: Twist 3 Back (sl 1 on cn, cnb, k2, p1 from cn).

T3F: Twist 3 Front (sl 2 on cn, cnf, p1, k2 from cn).

T4B: Twist 4 Back (sl 2 on cn, cnb, k2, p2 from cn).

T4F: Twist 4 Front (sl 2 on cn, cnf, p2, k2 from cn).

Note: Front and Back do not refer to the RS and WS of the fabric.

Stitch Patterns

1X1 RIBBING

Worked over a multiple of 2 sts; 1-row/rnd repeat.
Row/Rnd 1: *K1, p1; rep from * to end (around).
Rep Row/Rnd 1 as directed.

CHART 2: PANEL CHART A "DOUBLE MOSS STITCH"

Worked over a multiple of 4 sts; 4-row repeat.
Row 1 (RS): P1, k2, p1.
Row 2 (WS): K1, p2, k1.
Row 3: K1, p2, k1.
Row 4: P1, k2, p1.
Rep Rows 1-4 as directed.

CHART 3: PANEL CHART B "PILLAR CABLE"

Worked over a multiple of 5 sts; 2-row repeat.
Row 1 (RS): K1, [C2F] twice.
Row 2 (WS): P1, [C2BW] twice.
Rep Rows 1-2 as directed.

CHART 4: PANEL CHART C "STAGHORN CABLE"

Worked over a multiple of 16 sts; 6-row repeat.
Row 1 (RS): K4, C4B, C4F, k4.

Row 2 (WS): Purl all sts.
Row 3: K2, C4B, k4, C4F, k2.
Row 4: Rep Row 2.
Row 5: C4B, k8, C4F.
Row 6: Rep Row 2.
Rep Rows 1-6 as directed.

CHART 5: PANEL CHART D "INTERLOCKING CROSSES"

Worked over a multiple of 24 sts; 16-row repeat.
Row 1 (RS): P2, C4B, [p4, C4B] twice, p2.
Row 2 (WS): K2, p4, [k4, p4] twice, k2.
Row 3: P1, T3B, [T4F, T4B] twice, T3F, p1.
Row 4: K1, p2, k3, p4, k4, p4, k3, p2, k1.
Row 5: T3B, p3, C4F, p4, C4F, p3, T3F.
Row 6: P2, k4, [p4, k4] twice, p2.
Row 7: K2, p3, T3B, T4F, T4B, T3F, p3, k2.
Row 8: [P2, k3] twice, p4, [k3, p2] twice.
Row 9: [K2, p3] twice, C4B, [p3, k2] twice.
Row 10: Rep Row 8.
Row 11: K2, p3, T3F, T4B, T4F, T3B, p3, k2.
Row 12: Rep Row 6.
Row 13: T3F, p3, C4F, p4, C4F, p3, T3B.
Row 14: Rep Row 4.
Row 15: P1, T3F, [T4B, T4F] twice, T3B, p1.
Row 16: Rep Row 2.
Rep Rows 1-16 as directed.

CHART 6: PANEL E "REVERSE STOCKINETTE STITCH"

Worked over a multiple of 1 st; 2-row repeat.
Row 1 (RS): P1.
Row 2 (WS): K1.
Rep Rows 1-2 as directed.

CHART 7: PANEL F "12-STITCH BRAID"

Worked over a multiple of 12 sts; 8-row repeat.
Row 1 (RS): Knit all sts.
Row 2 (WS): Purl all sts.
Row 3: K4, C8B.
Row 4: Rep Row 2.
Row 5: Rep Row 1.
Row 6: Rep Row 2.
Row 7: C8F, K4.
Row 8: Rep Row 2.
Rep Rows 1-8 as directed.

Pattern Instructions

BACK

With smaller needles and using Channel Island cast-on method, CO 72 (84, 96, 108) sts. Work 1x1 Ribbing for 12 rows.

Switch to larger needles and work panel charts as shown in Chart 1 until back measures 13" (14¼", 15½", 16¼") [33 cm (36 cm, 39.5 cm, 41.5 cm)], or desired length to underarm, ending with a WS row.

Note: At this point you will stop working Panel Chart C (16 sts) and in its place work 4 repeats of Panel Chart A (4 sts). Continue to refer to Chart 1 for panel distribution.

Shape armholes as follows:

BO 4 (4, 5, 6) sts at beg of next 2 rows. 64 (76, 86, 96) sts on needles.

BO 3 sts at beg of next 2 rows. 58 (70, 80, 90) sts on needles.

Dec 1 st at beg and end of every RS row 3 (4, 5, 7) times. 52 (62, 70, 76) sts on needles.

Cont working in patt as est until armholes measure 7½" (8¾", 9¼", 10") [19 cm (22 cm, 23.5 cm, 25.5 cm)], ending with a WS row.

Shape shoulders as follows:
Cont working in patt as est and BO 7 (9, 7, 7) sts at beg of next 2 rows. 38 (44, 56, 62) sts on needles.

BO 6 (8, 6, 7) sts at beg of next 2 rows. 26 (28, 44, 48) sts on needles.

Sizes L (XL) only:
BO 6 (7) sts at beg of next 2 rows. 32 (34) sts on needles.

All sizes:
BO rem 26 (28, 32, 34) sts for back neck.

FRONT

With smaller needles and using Channel Island cast-on method, CO 72 (84, 96, 108) sts. Work 1x1 Ribbing for 12 rows.

Switch to larger needles and work panel charts as shown in Chart 1 until front measures same as back, ending with a WS row.

Note: At this point you will stop working the outer half of Panel Chart C (i.e., the 8 sts closest to the nearer side edge) and in its place work 2 repeats of Panel Chart A (4 sts). Continue to work the inner half of Panel Chart C as established (i.e., the 8 sts closest to center) and to refer to Chart 1 for panel distribution.

Shape armholes as follows:

BO 4 (4, 5, 6) sts at beg of next 2 rows. 64 (76, 86, 96) sts on needles.

BO 3 sts at beg of next 2 rows. 58 (70, 80, 90) sts on needles.

Dec 1 st at beg and end of every RS row 3 (4, 5, 7) times. 52 (62, 70, 76) sts on needles.

Cont working in patt as est until armholes measure 7¼" (8½", 9", 9¾") [18 cm (21 cm, 22.5 cm, 24.5 cm)], ending with a WS row.

Note: Neck and shoulder shaping are worked at the same time.

Shape front neck as follows:

With RS facing, work 19 (24, 27, 29) sts in patt.

Join new yarn and BO 14 (14, 16, 18) sts for front neck and work in patt to end. 19 (24, 27, 29) sts each side on needles.

Working each side separately, BO 2 (3, 3, 3) sts at each neck edge on next row and then BO 2 sts at each neck edge on foll row. 15 (19, 22, 24) sts each side on needles.

Work 1 WS row even.

Dec 1 st at each neck edge every RS row 2 (2, 3, 3) times while at the same time shaping shoulders as follows (final neck decreases will be worked while binding off):

BO 7 (9, 7, 7) sts at beg of next 2 rows at each armhole edge.

Then, BO 6 (8, 6, 7) sts at beg of foll 2 rows at each armhole edge.

Note: All sts have been bound off for Sizes S and M.

Sizes L (XL) only:

BO rem 6 (7) sts at beg of next 2 rows at each armhole edge.

SLEEVES (MAKE 2)

With smaller needles and using Channel Island cast-on method, CO 38 (40, 44, 46) sts. Work 1x1 Ribbing for 12 rows.

Switch to larger needles. Knit 1 row. Purl 1 row.

Establish patt as follows:

Row 1 (RS): K1 (2, 4, 5), [p2, k2] three times, work Chart 7, [k2, p2] three times, k to end.

Row 2 (WS): P1 (2, 4, 5), [k2, p2] three times, work Chart 7, [p2, k2] three times, p to end.

Row 3: K1 (2, 4, 5), [k2, p2] three times, work Chart 7, [p2, k2] three times, k to end.

Row 4: P1 (2, 4, 5), [p2, k2] three times, work Chart 7, [k2, p2] three times, p to end.

Cont working in patt as est and inc 1 st at beg and end of next row, then inc 1 st at beg and end of every 4th row, 0 (8, 9, 15) times and then inc 1 st at beg and end of every 6th row, 11 (7,

7, 3) times. 62 (72, 78, 84) sts on needles.

Cont working in patt as est until sleeve measures 16" (17", 18¼", 18½") [39.5 cm (42 cm, 45.5 cm, 46 cm)], or desired length to underarm, ending with a WS row.

Shape sleeve cap as follows:
Cont working in patt as est and BO 4 (4, 5, 6) sts at beg of next 2 rows. 54 (64, 68, 72) sts on needles.

BO 3 sts at beg of next 2 rows. 48 (58, 62, 66) sts on needles.

Dec 1 st at beg and end of every RS row 3 (4, 5, 7) times. 42 (50, 52, 52) sts on needles.

Then, dec 1 st at beg and end of every other RS row (i.e., every 4th row) 0 (1, 3, 2) time(s) and then dec 1 st at beg and end of every RS row 10 (8, 4, 6) times. 22 (32, 38, 36) sts on needles.

BO 2 sts at beg of next 0 (4, 2, 4) rows. 22 (24, 34, 28) sts on needles.

BO 5 (6, 9, 8) sts at beg of next 2 rows. 12 (12, 16, 12) sts on needles.

Size L only:
BO 2 sts at beg of next 2 rows. 12 sts on needles.

Work shoulder strap as follows:
Cont working Chart 7 as est until shoulder strap measures 3½" (4½", 5", 5¼") [9 cm (11.5 cm, 12.5 cm, 13.5 cm)] from last BO, ending with a WS row.

Place rem 12 sts on stitch holder or waste yarn and set aside.

FINISHING

Block pieces to finished measurements. With tapestry needle, sew front edges of sleeve caps to front armholes. Sew front edges of shoulder straps to BO edges of front shoulders. Sew back edges of sleeve caps to back armholes. Sew back edges of shoulder straps to BO edges of back shoulders. Sew sleeve and side seams. Weave in all loose ends with tapestry needle on the inside of the garment.

NECKBAND

With smaller needles and RS facing, knit 12 sts from right shoulder strap, pick up and knit 1 st for each BO st and 3 sts for every 4 rows around sloped edges around front neck, knit 12 sts from left shoulder strap, pick up and knit 1 st for each BO st at back neck.

Note: Total number of sts picked up must be even.

With RS facing, join in the rnd and pm to indicate EOR, being careful not to twist sts. Work 1x1 Ribbing for 24 rnds. BO all sts loosely using Icelandic bind-off method.

If desired, fold neckband in half and sew to the inside of the garment.

Katla
Women's Pullover
Chart 1: Panel Distribution Chart

GARMENT SIZE	PANEL DISTRIBUTION	STITCH COUNT
SIZE XL	A B A C A B A D A B A C A B A	108 sts
# of sts per panel	4 5 4 16 4 5 4 24 4 5 4 16 4 5 4	
SIZE L	E B A C A B E D E B A C A B E	96 sts
# of sts per panel	1 5 4 16 4 5 1 24 1 5 4 16 4 5 1	
SIZE M	A C A B E D E B A C A	84 sts
# of sts per panel	4 16 4 5 1 24 1 5 4 16 4	
SIZE S	E C E B E D E B E C E	72 sts
# of sts per panel	1 16 1 5 1 24 1 5 1 16 1	

Panel Legend
- A: Panel Chart A (4 sts)
- B: Panel Chart B (5 sts)
- C: Panel Chart C (16 sts)
- D: Panel Chart D (24 sts)
- E: Panel Chart E (1 st)

Color Legend
- ■ Size M: 9958 Light Indigo
- ■ Size XL: 9969 Fuchsia Heather

Katla
Women's Pullover
Chart 2: Panel Chart A
Double Moss Stitch

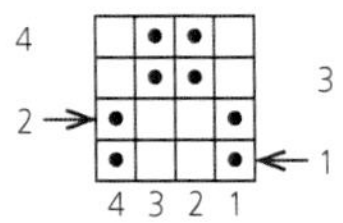

Stitch Legend
- □ K on RS, P on WS
- ⊡ P on RS, K on WS

Katla
Women's Pullover
Chart 3: Panel Chart B
Pillar Cable

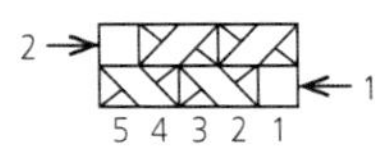

Stitch Legend
- □ K on RS, P on WS
- C2BW: Cross 2 Back on WS (sl 1 on cn, cnb, p1, p1 from cn)
- C2F: Cross 2 Front (sl 1 on cn, cnf, k1, k1 from cn)

Katla
Women's Pullover
Chart 4: Panel Chart C
Staghorn Cable

Stitch Legend

- K on RS, P on WS
- C4B: Cross 4 Back (sl 2 on cn, cnb, k2, k2 from cn)
- C4F: Cross 4 Front (sl 2 on cn, cnf, k2, k2 from cn)

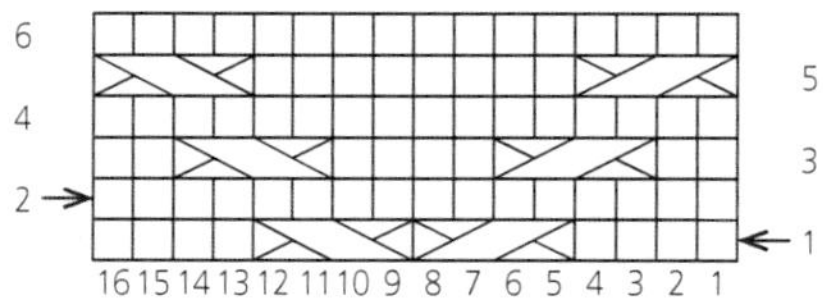

Katla
Women's Pullover
Chart 5: Panel Chart D
Interlocking Crosses

Stitch Legend

- K on RS, P on WS
- P on RS, K on WS
- T3B: Twist 3 Back (sl 1 on cn, cnb, k2, p1 from cn)
- T3F: Twist 3 Front (sl 2 on cn, cnf, p1, k2 from cn)
- C4B: Cross 4 Back (sl 2 on cn, cnb, k2, k2 from cn)
- C4F: Cross 4 Front (sl 2 on cn, cnf, k2, k2 from cn)
- T4B: Twist 4 Back (sl 2 on cn, cnb, k2, p2 from cn)
- T4F: Twist 4 Front (sl 2 on cn, cnf, p2, k2 from cn)

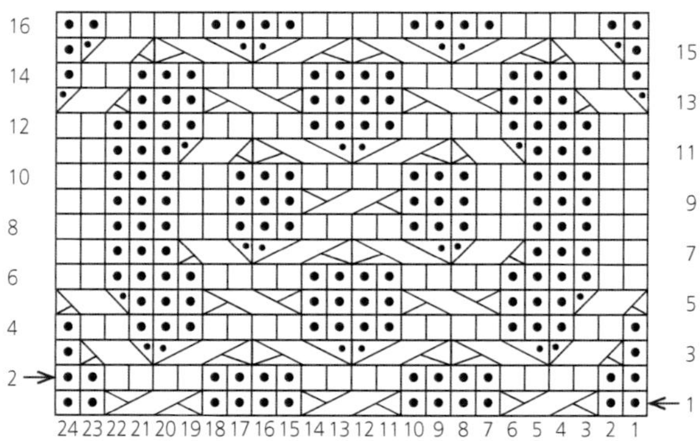

Katla
Women's Pullover
Chart 6: Panel Chart E
Reverse Stockinette Stitch

Stitch Legend

- P on RS, K on WS

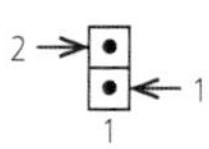

Katla
Women's Pullover
Chart 7: Panel Chart F
12-Stitch Braid

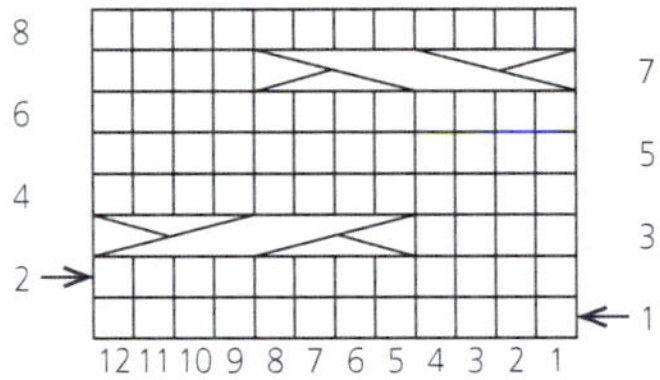

Stitch Legend

☐ K on RS, P on WS

C8B: Cross 8 Back (sl 4 on cn, cnb, k4, k4 from cn)

C8F: Cross 8 Front (sl 4 on cn, cnf, k4, k4 from cn)

Katla
Women's Pullover
Body Schematic

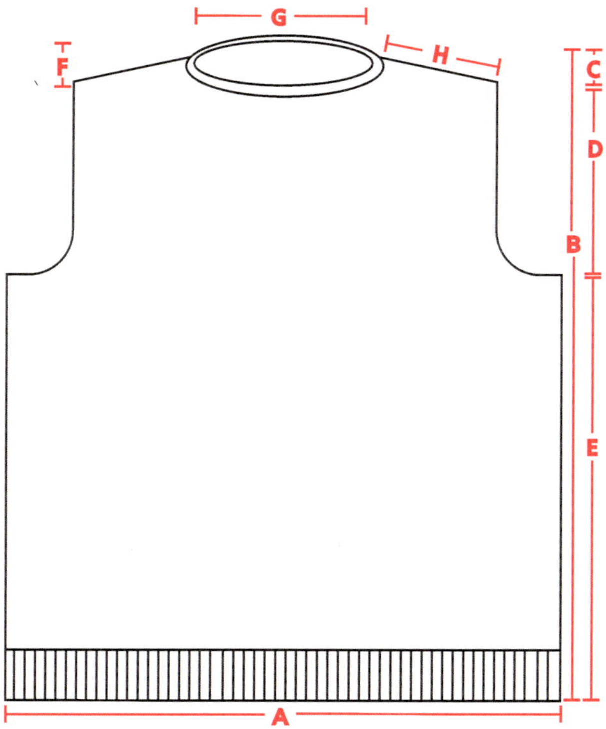

A BUST WIDTH:
18 (21, 24, 27) inches
45 (53, 60, 68) cm

B PULLOVER LENGTH:
21¾ (24¼, 26, 27½) inches
55 (61, 66, 70) cm

C SHOULDER DEPTH:
1¼ (1¼, 1¼, 1¼) inch
3 (3, 3, 3) cm

D ARMHOLE DEPTH:
7½ (8¾, 9¼, 10) inches
19 (22, 23.5, 25.5) cm

E BODY LENGTH:
13 (14¼, 15½, 16¼) inches
33 (36, 39.5, 41.5) cm

F NECK DEPTH:
1½ (1½, 1½, 1½) inches
4 (4, 4, 4) cm

G NECK WIDTH:
6½ (7, 8, 8½) inches
16.5 (17.5, 20, 21.5) cm

H SHOULDER WIDTH:
3½ (4½, 5, 5¼) inches
9 (11.5, 12.5, 13.5) cm

Katla
Women's Pullover
Sleeve Schematic

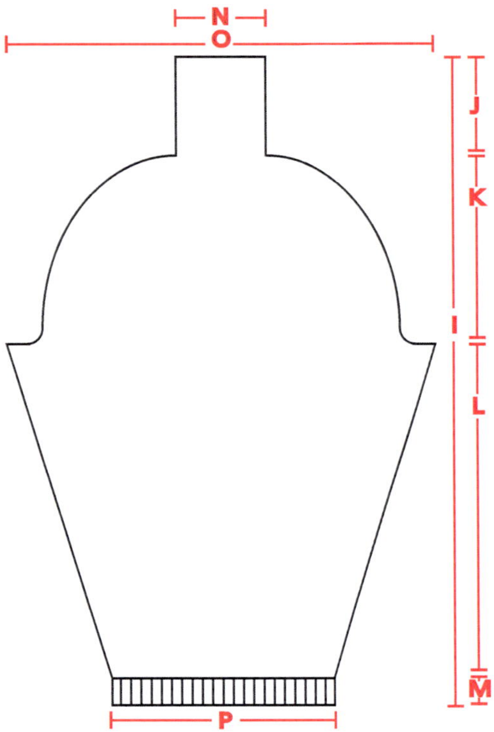

I SLEEVE LENGTH:
22½ (24½, 26¼, 27¼) inches
55.5 (61, 65.5, 68) cm

J SADDLE LENGTH:
3½ (4½, 5, 5¼) inches
9 (11.5, 12.5, 13.5) cm

K SLEEVE CAP LENGTH:
6½ (7½, 8, 8¾) inches
16 (19, 20, 22) cm

L ARM LENGTH:
13½ (14½, 15¾, 16) inches
33.5 (36, 39.5, 40) cm

M RIB LENGTH:
2½ (2½, 2½, 2½) inches
6 (6, 6, 6) cm

N SADDLE WIDTH:
2¾ (2¾, 2¾, 2¾) inches
6.5 (6.5, 6.5, 6.5) cm

O UPPER ARM CIRCUMFERENCE:
15½ (18, 19½, 21) inches
39 (45, 49, 52.5) cm

P CUFF CIRCUMFERENCE:
9½ (10, 11, 11½) inches
24 (25, 27.5, 29) cm

Hornstrandir

Hornstrandir is the designation of a nature reserve located on the northernmost part of Iceland's Westfjords peninsula. This area was widely inhabited until the middle of the twentieth century, when all of the farms and settlements were abandoned permanently. With no paved roads and only a few summerhouses remaining, Hornstrandir is a popular destination for adventure tourists looking to trek across its remote and desolate landscapes.

When I visited Ísafjörður a couple of summers ago, I would often sit on the jagged rocks that form the town's seawall and direct my gaze north towards Hornstrandir. For me, the view from that point perfectly captured my experiences in Iceland on that trip. This design is an attempt to recreate that view, first by employing a recursive basketweave stitch pattern to portray the choppy waves of the fjord and then by using a contrasting gray yarn to represent the rocky cliffs on the distant shore.

Project Overview

FINISHED MEASUREMENTS

Length: 69¾" [177 cm].
Width: 8" [20.5 cm].

YARN

Ístex Bulkylopi: 100% Icelandic wool; 66 yds [60 m] per 3.5 oz [100 g] skein.

- Color A: 9998 Atlantic Blue Shaded; 5 skeins.
- Color B: 0054 Light Ash Heather; 1 skein.

NEEDLES

US #13 [9.0 mm], or size needed to obtain gauge; 60" [150 cm] circular needles.

NOTIONS

Blunt tapestry needle.
Blocking pins, if desired.

GAUGE

9 sts and 16 rows = 4" [10 cm] in basketweave stitch, after blocking.

Gauge is not critical for this project, but differences in gauge will affect finished measurements and required yardage.

Construction Notes

This scarf is worked flat horizontally.

Directions for the Knitted Cast On and the Estonian Lace Bind Off, as well as other useful information, can be found in the Special Techniques section of the book.

Color A is the main color throughout the pattern; Color B is the contrasting color used only in Rows 29-32 and for the bind off.

Pattern Instructions

SCARF

Using Knitted cast-on method, CO 157 sts using Color A.

Row 1 (RS): *K1, p1; rep from * to last st, k1.
Rows 2-4: Rep Row 1 three times.

Row 5: K2tog, k1, p2, *k2, p2; rep from * to end. 156 sts on needles.
Row 6: *K2, p2; rep from * to end.

Row 7: *P2, k2; rep from * to end.
Row 8: Rep Row 7.

Row 9: *K4, p4; rep from * to last 4 sts, k4.
Row 10: P4, *k4, p4; rep from * to end.

Rows 11-12: Rep Rows 9-10.
Row 13: Rep Row 10.
Row 14: Rep Row 9.
Rows 15-16: Rep Rows 13-14.
Rows 17-20: Rep Rows 9-12.
Rows 21-22: Rep Rows 7-8.
Rows 23-24: Rep Row 6 twice.

Row 25: K1, k1fb, *p1, k1; rep from * to end. 157 sts on needles.

Rows 26-28: Rep Row 1 three times.
Rows 29-32: Rep Row 1 four times using Color B.

With Color B only, BO all sts using Estonian Lace bind-off method.

FINISHING

Weave in all loose ends with tapestry needle on the WS of the fabric. Block to finished measurements.

Winter Blueberries

Winter Blueberries started out as a simple experiment to see what a picot cast on would look like in a bulky yarn. Liking the result and wanting to build on it, I suddenly got the perverse idea to create a traditional Estonian Lace shawl out of Bulkylopi. I pulled out my copy of Nancy Bush's *Knitted Lace of Estonia* and created a veritable patchwork of stitch patterns, mirrored both horizontally and vertically.

I had always been intrigued by the Crown Prince Motif in Nancy Bush's book. On the surface, it is nothing more than a simple cross pattern surrounded by nupps. However, these nupps are arranged in such a way that they outline a large snowflake more suited to Scandinavian knitting than Estonian lace. Perhaps their use in the original shawl was a subtle nod to the Swedish roots of its recipient, after whom the motif was named.

The contrasting colorways used here inspired both the name of the shawl and the use of the blueberry stitch pattern. Using a super bulky yarn like Bulkylopi is a great way to learn knitted lace techniques, especially as the nupps in this pattern are produced from only 3 stitches. You will be able to create a treasured family heirloom in a fraction of the time it would take using a lace weight yarn and this design is guaranteed to keep you much warmer.

Project Overview

FINISHED MEASUREMENTS

Length: 62¾″ [159.5 cm].
Width: 15″ [38 cm].

YARN

Ístex Bulkylopi: 100% Icelandic wool; 66 yds [60 m] per 3.5 oz [100 g] skein.

- Color A: 0054 Light Ash Heather; 5 skeins.
- Color B: 9998 Atlantic Blue Shaded; 3 skeins.

NEEDLES

US #13 [9.0 mm], or size needed to obtain gauge; 60″ [150 cm] circular needles.

NOTIONS

8 stitch markers
Blunt tapestry needle.
Blocking pins, if desired.

GAUGE

10 sts and 16 rows = 4″ [10 cm] in blueberry stitch, after blocking.

Gauge is not critical for this project, but differences in gauge will affect finished measurements and required yardage.

Construction Notes

This shawl is worked flat horizontally.

Directions for the Picot Cast On and the Estonian Lace Bind Off, as well as other useful information, can be found in the Special Techniques section of the book.

Slip all markers unless otherwise directed.

When slipping the first stitch of a row, slip the stitch purlwise with yarn in front.

When slipping a stitch to work a decrease [sl 1, k2tog, psso], slip the stitch knitwise with yarn in back.

All WS stitches are purled except for the 4-st garter stitch border at the beginning and the end of each row and the [p3tog] nupps.

Color A is the main color throughout the pattern; Color B is the contrasting color used only in Rows 11–28 of the Center Sections.

Stitch Patterns

CHART 1: BEGINNING BLUEBERRY STITCH

Worked over a multiple of 4 sts; 4-row repeat.
Row 1 (RS): *[Sl 1, k2tog, psso], [k1, yo, k1] in 1 st; rep from * across.
Row 2 (WS): Purl all sts.
Row 3: *[K1, yo, k1] in 1 st, [sl 1 k2tog, psso]; rep from * across.
Row 4: Rep Row 2.
Rep Rows 1-4 as directed.

CHART 2: CENTER PANEL

Worked over 5 sts; 4-row repeat.
Row 1 (RS): [Sl 1, k1, psso], yo, k1, yo, k2tog.
Row 2 (WS): Purl all sts.
Rows 3-4: Rep Rows 1-2.
Rep Rows 1-4 as directed.

CHART 3: ENDING BLUEBERRY STITCH

Worked over a multiple of 4 sts; 4-row repeat.
Row 1 (RS): *[K1, yo, k1] in 1 st, [sl 1, k2tog, psso]; rep from * across.
Row 2 (WS): Purl all sts.
Row 3: *[Sl 1, k2tog, psso], [k1, yo, k1] in 1 st; rep from * across.
Row 4: Rep Row 2.
Rep Rows 1-4 as directed.

CHART 4: CROWN PRINCE MOTIF

Worked over 19 sts and 38 rows.

Row 1 (RS): K4, [k1, yo, k1] in 1 st, k9, [k1, yo, k1] in 1 st, k4.

Row 2 (WS): p4, p3tog, p9, p3tog, p4.

Row 3: K4, *[k1, yo, k1] in 1 st; rep from * once, k7, *[k1, yo, k1] in 1 st; rep from * once, k4.

Row 4: P4, *p3tog; rep from * once, p7, *p3tog; rep from * once, p4.

Row 5: K4, [k1, yo, k1] in 1 st, k1, [k1, yo, k1] in 1 st, k5, [k1, yo, k1] in 1 st, k1, [k1, yo, k1] in 1 st, k4.

Row 6: P4, p3tog, p1, p3tog, p5, p3tog, p1, p3tog, p4.

Row 7: K4, [k1, yo, k1] in 1 st, k2, [k1, yo, k1] in 1 st, k3, [k1, yo, k1] in 1 st, k2, [k1, yo, k1] in 1 st, k4.

Row 8: P4, p3tog, p2, p3tog, p3, p3tog, p2, p3tog, p4.

Row 9: *[K1, yo, k1] in 1 st; rep from * three times, k1, yo, [sl 1, k1, psso], k1, [k1, yo, k1] in 1 st, k1, [k1, yo, k1] in 1 st, k2tog, yo, k1, *[k1, yo, k1] in 1 st; rep from * three times.

Row 10: *P3tog; rep from * three times, p4, p3tog, p1, p3tog, p4, *p3tog; rep from * three times.

Row 11: K1, [k1, yo, k1] in 1 st, k2, yo, [sl 1, k1, psso], yo, [sl 1, k1, psso], k1, [k1, yo, k1] in 1 st, k1, k2tog, yo, k2tog, yo, k2, [k1, yo, k1] in 1 st, k1.

Row 12: P1, p3tog, p7, p3tog, p7, p3tog, p1.

Row 13: K2, [k1, yo, k1] in 1 st, k2, yo, [sl 1, k1, psso], yo, [sl 1, k1, psso], k1, k2tog, yo, k2tog, yo, k2, [k1, yo, k1] in 1 st, k2.

Row 14: p2, p3tog, p13, p3tog, p2.

Row 15: K3, [k1, yo, k1] in 1 st, k2, yo, [sl 1, k1, psso], yo, [sl 1, k2tog, psso], yo, k2tog, yo, k2, [k1, yo, k1] in 1 st, k3.

Row 16: P3, p3tog, p11, p3tog, p3.

Row 17: K4, [k1, yo, k1] in 1 st, k2, yo, [sl 1, k1, psso], k1, k2tog, yo, k2, [k1, yo, k1] in 1 st, k4.

Row 18: P4, p3tog, p9, p3tog, p4.

Row 19: K5, [k1, yo, k1] in 1 st, k2, yo, [sl 1, k2tog, psso], yo, k2, [k1, yo, k1] in 1 st, k5.

Row 20: P5, p3tog, p7, p3tog, p5.

Row 21: K4, [k1, yo, k1] in 1 st, k1, k2tog, yo, k3, yo, [sl 1, k1, psso], k1, [k1, yo, k1] in 1 st, k4.

Row 22: P4, p3tog, p9, p3tog, p4.

Row 23: K3, [k1, yo, k1] in 1 st, k1, k2tog, yo, k2tog, yo, k1, yo, [sl 1, k1, psso], yo, [sl 1, k1, psso], k1, [k1, yo, k1] in 1 st, k3.

Row 24: P3, p3tog, p11, p3tog, p3.

Row 25: K2, [k1, yo, k1] in 1 st, k1, k2tog, yo, k2tog, yo, k3, yo, [sl 1, k1, psso], yo, [sl 1, k1, psso], k1, [k1, yo, k1] in 1 st, k2.

Row 26: P2, p3tog, p13, p3tog, p2.

Row 27: K1, [k1, yo, k1] in 1 st, k1, k2tog, yo, k2tog, yo, k2, [k1, yo, k1] in 1 st, k2, yo, [sl 1, k1, psso], yo, [sl 1, k1, psso], k1, [k1, yo, k1] in 1 st, k1.

Row 28: P1, p3tog, p7, p3tog, p7, p3tog, p1.

Row 29: *[K1, yo, k1] in 1 st; rep from * three times, k2tog, yo, k2, [k1, yo, k1] in 1 st, k1, [k1, yo, k1] in 1 st, k2, yo, [sl 1, k1, psso], *[k1, yo, k1] in 1 st; rep from * three times.

Row 30: *P3tog; rep from * three times, p4, p3tog, p1, p3tog, p4, *p3tog; rep from * three times.

Row 31: Rep Row 7.
Row 32: Rep Row 8.
Row 33: Rep Row 5.
Row 34: Rep Row 6.
Row 35: Rep Row 3.
Row 36: Rep Row 4.
Row 37: Rep Row 1.
Row 38: Rep Row 2.

CHART 5: NUPP SQUARES MOTIF

Worked over 6 sts; 4-row repeat.
Row 1 (RS): *K1, [k1, yo, k1] in 1 st, k1; rep from * once.
Row 2 (WS): *P1, p3tog, p1; rep from * once.
Row 3: Knit all sts.
Row 4: Purl all sts.
Rep Rows 1-4 as directed.

Pattern Instructions

GARTER STITCH FRAME

Using Picot cast-on method, CO 157 sts using Color A.

Set-Up Row 1 (RS): K4, pm, k72, pm, k5, pm, k72, pm, k4.

Set-Up Row 2 (WS): Knit all sts.

BOTTOM BLUEBERRY STITCH BORDER

Row 1 (RS): Sl 1 wyif, k3, sl m, work Row 1 of Chart 1 to next marker, work Row 1 of Chart 2, sl m, work Row 1 of Chart 3 to next marker, k4.
Row 2 (WS): Sl 1 wyif, k3, purl to last 4 sts, k4.

Row 3: As Row 1, working Row 3 of all charts.
Row 4: Rep Row 2.
Rows 5-7: Rep Rows 1-3.
Row 8: Sl 1 wyif, k3, p8, pm, p56, pm, p21, pm, p56, pm, p8, k4.

Note: There should be a total of 8 stitch markers on the needles at this point.

CENTER SECTIONS

Row 1 (RS): Sl 1 wyif, k3, sl m, work Row 1 of Chart 1 to next marker, *k6, work Row 1 of Chart 4; rep from * once, k6, sl m, work Row 1 of Chart 1 to next marker, work Row 1 of Chart 2, sl m, work Row 1 of Chart 3 to next marker, *k6, work Row 1 of Chart 4; rep from * once, k6, sl m, work Row 1 of Chart 3 to next marker, k4.

Row 2 (WS): Sl 1 wyif, k3, p8, *p6, work Row 2 of Chart 4; rep from * once, p6, p21, *p6, work Row 2 of Chart 4; rep from * once, p6, purl to last 4 sts, k4.

Rows 3-10: Work 8 rows in patt as est.

Rows 11-16: Cut Color A. Using Color B, work 6 rows in patt as est.

Row 17: Sl 1 wyif, k3, sl m, work Row 1 of Chart 1 to next marker, *work Row 1 of Chart 5, work Row 17 of Chart 4; rep from * once, work Row 1 of Chart 5, sl m, work Row 1 of Chart 1 to next marker, work Row 1 of Chart 2, sl m, work Row 1 of Chart 3 to next marker, *work Row 1 of Chart 5, work Row 17 of Chart 4; rep from * once, work Row 1 of Chart 5, sl m, work Row 1 of Chart 3 to next marker, k4.

Row 18: Sl 1 wyif, k3, p8, *work Row 2 of Chart 5, work Row 18 of Chart 4; rep from * once, work Row 2 of Chart 5, p21, *work Row 2 of Chart 5, work Row 18 of Chart 4; rep from * once, work Row 2 of Chart 5, purl to last 4 sts, k4.

Rows 19-24: Work 6 rows in patt as est, repeating 4-row charts.

Rows 25-28: Rep Rows 1-2 twice, working applicable rows of Chart 4.

Rows 29-38: Cut Color B. Using Color A, work 10 rows in patt as est.

TOP BLUEBERRY STITCH BORDER

Row 1 (RS): Sl 1 wyif, k3, sl m, work Row 3 of Chart 1 to 4th marker, removing 2nd and 3rd markers along the way, work Row 3 of Chart 2, sl m, work Row 3 of Chart 3 to 8th marker, removing 6th and 7th markers along the way, k4.

Row 2 (WS): Sl 1 wyif, k3, purl to last 4 sts, k4.

Row 3: As Row 1, working Row 1 of all charts.

Row 4: Rep Row 2.
Rows 5-8: Rep Rows 1-4.

GARTER STITCH FRAME

Purl 2 rows, removing markers.

Set-Up Row 1 (RS): K1, *yo, k2tog; rep from * thirty-seven times, yo, [sl 1, k2tog, psso], yo, *k2tog, yo; rep from * to last st, k1.

Set-Up Row 2 (WS): Purl all sts.

BO all sts using Estonian Lace bind-off method.

FINISHING

Weave in all loose ends with tapestry needle on the WS of the fabric. Block to finished measurements.

Winter Blueberries Unisex Shawl Chart 1: Panel Chart A Beginning Blueberry Stitch

Stitch Legend

- Knit on RS , Purl on WS
- [Sl 1, k2tog, psso]
- [K1, yo, k1] in 1 st
- No Stitch

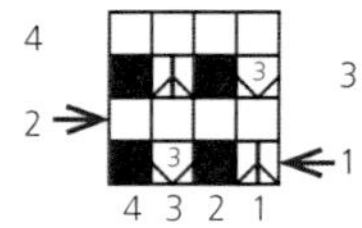

Winter Blueberries Unisex Shawl Chart 2: Panel Chart B Center Panel

Stitch Legend

- Knit on RS , Purl on WS
- [Sl 1, k1, psso]
- K2tog
- Yarn over

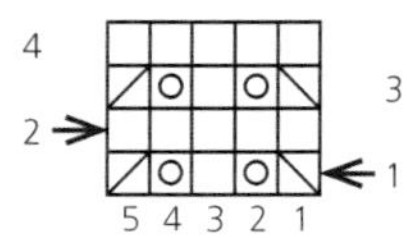

Winter Blueberries Unisex Shawl Chart 3: Panel Chart C Ending Blueberry Stitch

Stitch Legend

- Knit on RS , Purl on WS
- [Sl 1, k2tog, psso]
- [K1, yo, k1] in 1 st
- No Stitch

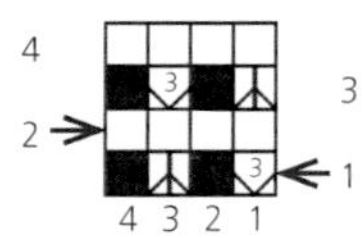

Winter Blueberries Unisex Shawl
Chart 4: Panel Chart D
Crown Prince Motif

Stitch Legend

□	Knit on RS, Purl on WS
P3tog symbol	P3tog
[K1, yo, k1] symbol	[K1, yo, k1] in 1 st
[Sl 1, k2tog, psso] symbol	[Sl 1, k2tog, psso]
[Sl 1, k1, psso] symbol	[Sl 1, k1, psso]
K2tog symbol	K2tog
○	Yarn Over

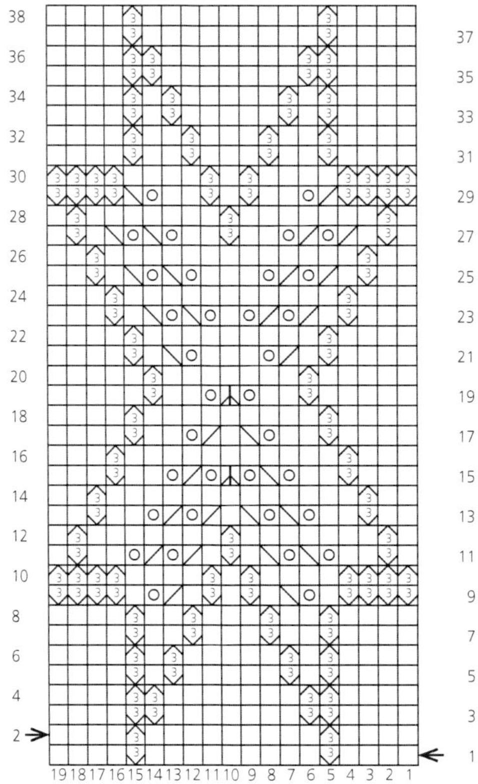

Winter Blueberries Unisex Shawl
Chart 5: Panel Chart E
Nupp Squares Motif

Stitch Legend

□	Knit on RS, Purl on WS
P3tog symbol	P3tog
[K1, yo, k1] symbol	[K1, yo, k1] in 1 st

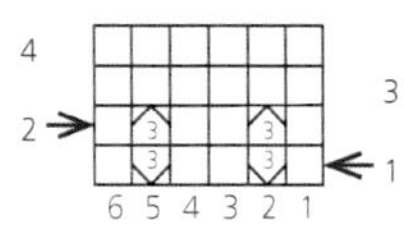

Westfjords

The Westfjords region in the northwest of Iceland possesses some of the most beautiful vistas that I have ever seen. Descending by airplane into Ísafjörður can be a little unnerving, but it does provide you with the best views of this dramatic landscape. Sitting on a spit of land in the middle of a fjord, the town is flanked on both sides by mountains that rise up directly from the water.

I had been lured to Ísafjörður by a Sigur Rós video, and it was there, on a bright summer's day in its quaint town square, that I cast on for this hat. Days earlier, I had picked up a few skeins of Einband for the first time in Reykjavík. I was particularly enchanted by the teal colorway, as it is not available in any of the other weights of Lopi yarn and I was eager to start a new project.

Inspired by my surroundings, I came up with a design that makes use of gradient stripes to reflect the subtle changes in the color of the fjord. The farther out I looked, the deeper the water became and I tried to replicate this effect by gradually shifting from the teal to navy. With its brim turned up, the hat also captures my memory of the light gray foam washing up onto the dark gray sand of the shoreline. The teal and the grays at the crown are suggestive of the clear blue sky and the imposing glaciers that guard the town from a distance.

Project Overview

SIZES

S (M, L) to fit head circumference of 18" (20", 22") [45.5 cm (51 cm, 56 cm)]. with ½-1¼" [1-3.5 cm] positive ease intended.

Shown in Size L with ½" [1 cm] of positive ease.

FINISHED MEASUREMENTS

Head Circumference: 19¼" (20¾", 22½") [49 cm (52.5 cm, 57 cm)].

Height from Brim to Crown: 11" (11¼", 11½")].

YARN

Ístex Einband: 100% wool; 273 yds [250 m] per 1.75 oz [50 g] skein

- Color A: 1027 Light Grey Heather; 1 skein for all sizes.
- Color B: 9103 Dark Grey Heather; 1 skein for all sizes.
- Color C: 1761 Teal; 1 skein for all sizes.
- Color D: 0118 Navy; 1 skein for all sizes.

NEEDLES

US #2 [2.75 mm], or size needed to obtain gauge;

- All sizes: 16" [40 cm] circular needles.
- Optional: double-pointed needles for small-circumference knitting.

Note: Begin with circular needles to accommodate the cast-on stitches for the brim. Use your preferred method of small-circumference knitting to work the crown.

NOTIONS

1 stitch marker (to indicate end of round).
Blunt tapestry needle.
Blocking pins, if desired.

GAUGE

30 sts and 42 rnds = 4" [10 cm] in St st, after blocking.

Construction Notes

This hat is worked seamlessly in the round from the bottom up.

Directions for the Knitted Cast On, as well as other useful information, can be found in the Special Techniques section of the book.

Stitch Patterns

2X2 RIBBING

Worked over a multiple of 4 sts; 1-rnd repeat.
Rnd 1: *K2, p2; rep from * around.
Rep Rnd 1 as directed.

Pattern Instructions

BRIM

Using Knitted cast-on method, CO 144 (156, 168) sts using Color A. Join in the rnd and pm to indicate EOR, being careful not to twist sts.

Work 2x2 Ribbing for 4 rnds using Color A.

Work 2x2 Ribbing for 8 rnds using Color B.

BODY

Knit 12 rnds using Color B.
Knit 15 rnds using Color C.
Knit 1 rnd using Color D.
Knit 5 rnds using Color C.
Knit 2 rnds using Color D.
Knit 4 rnds using Color C.
Knit 3 rnds using Color D.
Knit 3 rnds using Color C.
Knit 4 rnds using Color D.
Knit 2 rnds using Color C.
Knit 5 rnds using Color D.
Knit 1 rnd using Color C.
Knit 15 rnds using Color D.
Knit 3 rnds using Color B.
Knit 1 rnd using Color A.
Knit 2 rnds using Color B.
Knit 2 rnds using Color A.
Knit 1 rnd using Color B.
Knit 3 rnds using Color A.

CROWN

Using Color C, work decreases as follows, changing to preferred needles for small-circumference knitting when necessary:

Size L only:
*K12, k2tog; rep from * around.
156 sts on needles.
Knit all sts.

Sizes M and L only:
*K11, k2tog; rep from * around.
144 sts on needles.
Knit all sts.

All sizes:
*K10, k2tog; rep from * around.
132 sts on needles.
Knit all sts.

*K9, k2tog; rep from * around.
120 sts on needles.
Knit all sts.

*K8, k2tog; rep from * around.
108 sts on needles.
Knit all sts.

*K7, k2tog; rep from * around.
96 sts on needles.
Knit all sts.

*K6, k2tog; rep from * around.
84 sts on needles.
Knit all sts.

*K5, k2tog; rep from * around.
72 sts on needles.
Knit all sts.

*K4, k2tog; rep from * around.
60 sts on needles.
Knit all sts.

*K3, k2tog; rep from * around.
48 sts on needles.
Knit all sts.

*K2, k2tog; rep from * around.
36 sts on needles.
Knit all sts.

*K1, k2tog; rep from * around.
24 sts on needles.
Knit all sts.

*K2tog; rep from * around.
12 sts on needles.

Cut working yarn and pull tightly through rem sts.

FINISHING

Weave in all loose ends with tapestry needle on the inside of the hat. Block to finished measurements.

Monsina

Monsina was my mother's middle name and the last sweater in this book is dedicated to her. The name originated with our Norwegian ancestors, although it is spelled "Monsine" in the historical records. I had intended for this pullover to be a cropped, allover Fair Isle design with striped three-quarter sleeves. Just as I got to the yoke divide, however, my mother passed away peacefully after a long illness. All I could do at this point was knit one round after another in a single color, or as I called it at the time, my "stockinette of grief." Whenever I look at this sweater now, though, it reminds me of her and how proud she was of me that I was writing a book of my own.

This pullover is worked using Einband held double-stranded. One of the nice features of this laceweight version of Lopi is the bounty of beautiful colors that are not available in its other weights. Garter Stitch rows at the neck are rolled over and sewn to the inside, which allow the Fair Isle bands of the garment to begin immediately. Sleeve decreases begin rather late at the elbow, after the striping, which create an unusual silhouette, an adjective that most definitely described my mother. To be fair, the apple didn't fall too far from the tree.

Project Overview (Women's Pullover)

SIZES

XS (S, M, L, XL, XXL) to fit bust circumference of 34" (38", 42", 46", 50", 54") [86.5 cm (96.5 cm, 106.5 cm, 117 cm, 127 cm, 137 cm)] with 3-3¾" [5.5-7.5 cm] of positive ease intended.

Women's Pullover not shown.

Note: Women's Pullover has one less yoke chart repeat than Men's Pullover.

FINISHED MEASUREMENTS

Bust Circumference: 37½" (41", 45½", 49", 53½", 57¾") [93.5 cm (102.5 cm, 113.5 cm, 122.5 cm, 133.5 cm, 144.5 cm)].

Pullover Length: 22" (22¾", 23¼", 24", 24¾", 25¼") [55.5 cm (57 cm, 59 cm, 60.5 cm, 62 cm, 64 cm)].

YARN

Ístex Einband: 100% Icelandic wool; 273 yds [250 m] per 1.75 oz [50 g] skein.

- Color A: 9142 Fuchsia; 2 skeins for all sizes.
- Color B: 9281 Sky Blue; 2 skeins for all sizes.
- Color C: 9028 Citron; 2 skeins for all sizes.
- Color D: 9044 Purple; 2 skeins for all sizes.
- Color E: 9277 Royal Blue; 2 (2, 2, 4, 4, 4) skeins.
- Color F: 1768 Pink; 2 skeins for all sizes.
- Color G: 1764 Vivid Green; 2 skeins for all sizes.
- Color H: 0851 White; 2 skeins for all sizes.
- Color I: 1761 Teal; 4 (4, 4, 6, 6, 6) skeins.
- Color J: 9128 Blush; 2 skeins for all sizes.
- Color K: 1762 Turquoise; 2 skeins for all sizes.
- Color L: 1769 Cherry; 2 skeins for all sizes.

NEEDLES

US #6 [4.0 mm], or size needed to obtain gauge;

- All sizes: 24" [60 cm], 32" [80 cm], and 40" [100 cm] circular needles.

- Sizes XL-XXL: 60" [150 cm] circular needles.
- Optional: double-pointed needles for small-circumference knitting.

Note: Begin with the shortest circular needles and switch to longer lengths as needed while working the yoke. Use your preferred method of small-circumference knitting to work the sleeves.

NOTIONS

1 stitch marker (to indicate end of round).

2 short circular stitch holders or waste yarn (to hold live stitches for sleeves).

Blunt tapestry needle.
Blocking pins, if desired.

GAUGE

22 sts and 24 rnds = 4" [10 cm] in St st with yarn held double-stranded, after blocking.

Construction Notes

This garment is worked seamlessly in the round from the top down.

Directions for the Knitted Cast On and Jeny's Surprisingly Stretchy Bind Off, as well as other useful information, can be found in the Special Techniques section of the book.

The garter stitch neckband is worked flat, then the yoke is knit in the round with increases occurring before and after each band of stranded colorwork.

The yoke is then divided to work the body, with additional stitches cast on at the underarms, while the sleeve stitches are held separately.

The sleeves are worked from the upper arm down with stitches picked up from the cast-on edge at the underarms and are tapered with decreases below the elbow.

3x3 Ribbing is worked at the hem and the cuffs.

Yarn is held double-stranded throughout.

Stitch Patterns

3X3 RIBBING

Worked over a multiple of 6 sts; 1-rnd repeat.
Rnd 1: *K3, p3; rep from * around.
Rep Rnd 1 as directed.

Pattern Instructions

YOKE

Using Knitted cast-on method, CO 90 (99, 108, 108, 117, 117) sts using Color A. Do not join. Knit 8 rows flat. With RS facing, join in the rnd and pm to indicate EOR, being careful not to twist sts. Knit 2 rnds.

Work Rnds 1-7 of Chart 1 with Colors A, B, C and D, repeating to EOR. Cut Colors B, C and D. With Color A only, knit 1 rnd even. Knit 1 rnd, inc 0 (1, 0, 0, 1, 1) st(s). 90 (100, 108, 108, 118, 118) sts on needles. Cut Color A.

With Color E only, work Inc Rnd 1: *K2, M1; rep from * around. 135 (150, 162, 162, 177, 177) sts on needles. Knit 1 rnd, inc 0 (3, 0, 0, 3, 3) sts evenly. 135 (153, 162, 162, 180, 180) sts on needles.

Work Rnds 1-9 of Chart 2 with Colors E, F, G and H, repeating to EOR. Cut Colors, F, G and H. With Color E only, knit 1 rnd even. Knit 1 rnd, inc 1 (1, 0, 0, 0, 0) st(s). 136 (154, 162, 162, 180, 180) sts on needles. Cut Color E.

With Color A only, work Inc Rnd 2: *K2, M1; rep from * around. 204 (231, 243, 243, 270, 270) sts on needles. Knit 1 rnd, inc 3 (3, 0, 0, 0, 0) sts evenly. 207 (234, 243, 243, 270, 270) sts on needles.

Work Rnds 1-7 of Chart 1 with Colors A, B, C and D, repeating to EOR. Cut Colors B, C and D. With Color A only, knit 2 rnds. Cut Color A.

With Color I only, work Inc Rnd 3: *K3, M1; rep from * around. 276 (312, 324, 324, 360, 360) sts on needles.

Size S only:
Knit 1 rnd, dec 6 sts evenly. 306 sts on needles.

All other sizes:
Knit 1 rnd, inc 12 (-, 0, 18, 0, 18) sts evenly. 288 (- , 324, 342, 360, 378) sts on needles.

Work Rnds 1-15 of Chart 3 with Colors G, H, I, J, K and L, repeating to EOR. Cut Colors G, H, J, K and L.

With Color I only, knit 1 rnd even. Knit 1 rnd, dec 30 (24, 18, 12, 6, 0) sts evenly. 258 (282, 306, 330, 354, 378) sts on needles. Knit 0 (1, 2, 3, 4, 5) rnd(s).

BODY

Divide body and sleeves from yoke as follows:

With Color I only, *knit 83 (91, 99, 107, 115, 125) sts (front/back). Place next 46 (50, 54, 58, 62, 64) sts (sleeve) on circular stitch holder or waste yarn. Using Knitted cast-on method, CO 20 (22, 26, 28, 32, 34) sts for underarm. Rep from * once, then pm to indicate EOR. 206 (226, 250, 270, 294, 318) sts on needles.

Work in St st until body measures 10" (10½", 11", 11½", 12", 12½") [25.5 cm (26.5 cm,

28 cm, 29 cm, 30.5 cm, 32 cm)], or 3″ [7.5 cm] less than desired length to hem.

Work 3x3 Ribbing for 18 rnds. BO all sts loosely using Jeny's Surprisingly Stretchy bind-off method.

SLEEVES (MAKE 2)

Using preferred method of small-circumference knitting, beg at center of underarm with RS facing, join Color I and pick up and knit 10 (11, 13, 14, 16, 17) sts from CO sts at underarm, pick up and knit 1 st in gap between body and sleeve, knit 46 (50, 54, 58, 62, 64) sleeve sts from circular stitch holder or waste yarn, pick up and knit 1 st between body and sleeve, then pick up and knit rem 10 (11, 13, 14, 16, 17) from underarm CO edge. 68 (74, 82, 88, 96, 100) sts on needles.

Join in the rnd and pm to indicate EOR, being careful not to twist sts. Knit 2 rnds.

Cut Color I. With Color K only, knit 3 rnds. With Color G, knit 1 rnd.

Cut Color G. With Color K only, knit 3 rnds.
Cut Color K. With Color I only, knit 6 rnds.
Cut Color I. With Color A only, knit 4 rnds.
Cut Color A. With Color C only, knit 3 rnds.
Cut Color C. With Color A only, knit 4 rnds.
Cut Color A. With Color E only, knit 5 rnds.
Cut Color E. With Color G only, knit 3 rnds.
Cut Color G. With Color E only, knit 5 rnds.
Cut Color E. With Color A only, knit 4 rnds.
Cut Color A. With Color C only, knit 3 rnds.
Cut Color C. With Color A only, knit 4 rnds.

Cut Color A.

With Color E only, work in St st and dec 1 st at beg and end of every 2nd rnd, 7 (10,11, 14, 15, 17) times. 54 (54, 60, 60, 66, 66) sts on needles.

Work in St st until sleeve measures 13¼″ (14″, 14¾″, 15″, 15½″, 16″) [33.5 cm (35.5 cm, 37.5 cm, 38 cm, 39.5 cm, 40.5 cm)], or 3″ [7.5 cm] less than desired length to cuff.

Work 3x3 Ribbing for 18 rnds. BO all sts loosely using Jeny's Surprisingly Stretchy bind-off method.

NECKBAND

Sew ends together. Fold neckband in half and sew to the inside of the garment.

FINISHING

Weave in all loose ends with tapestry needle on the inside of the garment. Block to finished measurements.

Monsina
Men's and Women's Pullovers
Chart 1: Yoke Chart A

Color Legend

- Knit with Color A: 9142 Fuchsia
- Knit with Color B: 9281 Sky Blue
- Knit with Color C: 9028 Citron
- Knit with Color D: 9044 Purple

Monsina
Men's and Women's Pullovers
Chart 2: Yoke Chart B

Color Legend

- Knit with Color E: 9277 Royal Blue
- Knit with Color F: 1768 Pink
- Knit with Color G: 1764 Vivid Green
- Knit with Color H: 0851 White

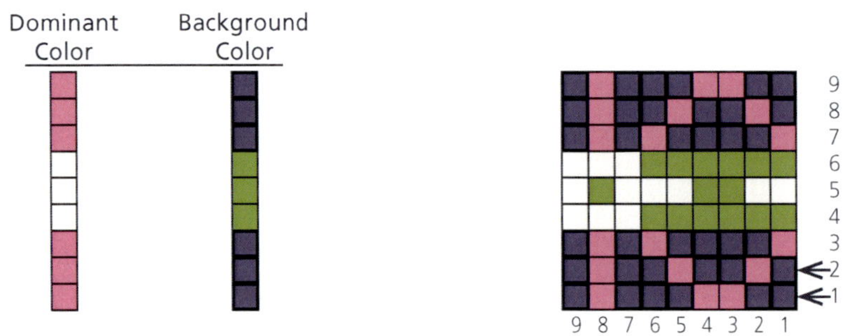

Monsina
Men's and Women's Pullovers
Chart 3: Yoke Chart C

Color Legend

- Knit with Color G: 1764 Vivid Green
- Knit with Color H: 0851 White
- Knit with Color I: 1761 Teal
- Knit with Color J: 9128 Blush
- Knit with Color K: 1762 Turquoise
- Knit with Color L: 1769 Cherry

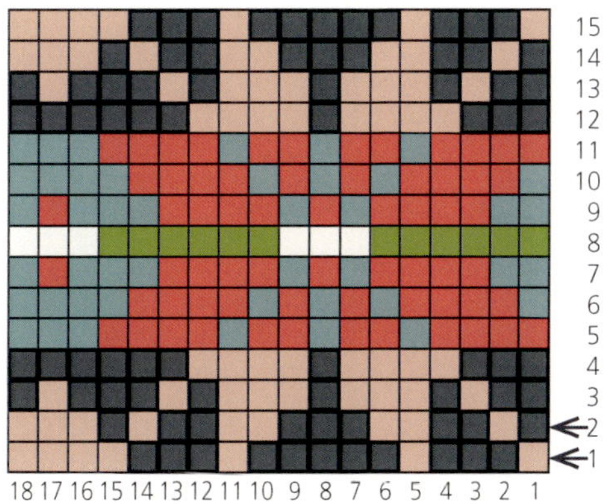

Monsina Women's Pullover Schematic

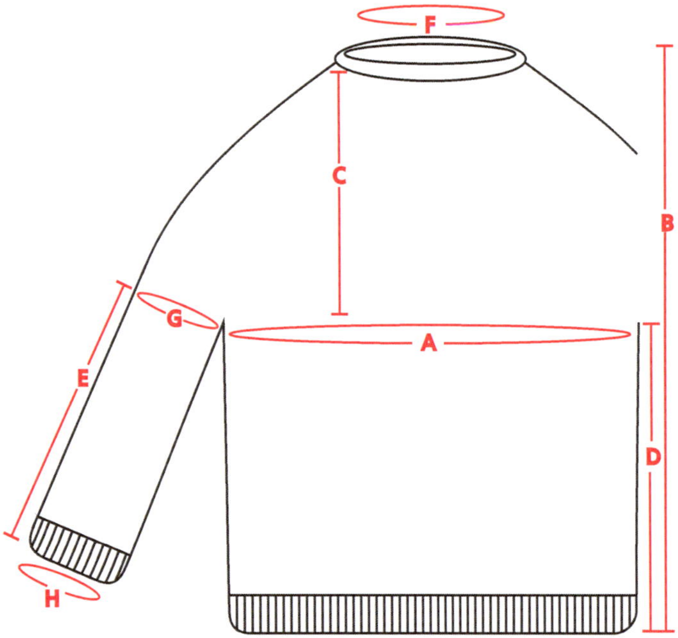

A BUST CIRCUMFERENCE:
37½ (41, 45½, 49, 53½, 57¾) inches
93.5 (102.5, 113.5, 122.5, 133.5, 144.5) cm

B PULLOVER LENGTH:
22 (22¾, 23¼, 24, 24¾, 25¼) inches
55.5 (57, 59, 60.5, 62, 64) cm

C YOKE DEPTH:
9 (9¼, 9¼, 9½, 9½, 9¾) inches
22.5 (23, 23.5, 24, 24, 24.5) cm

D BODY LENGTH:
13 (13½, 14, 14½, 15, 15½) inches
33 (34, 35.5, 36.5, 38, 39.5) cm

E SLEEVE LENGTH:
16¼ (17, 17¾, 18, 18½, 19) inches
41 (43, 45, 45.5, 47, 48) cm

F NECK CIRCUMFERENCE:
16¼ (18, 19¾, 19¾, 21¼, 21¼) inches
41 (45, 49, 49, 53, 53) cm

G UPPER ARM CIRCUMFERENCE:
12¼ (13½, 15, 16, 17½, 18) inches
31 (33.5, 37.5, 40, 44.5, 45.5) cm

H CUFF CIRCUMFERENCE:
9¾ (9¾, 11, 11, 12, 12) inches
24.5 (24.5, 27.5, 27.5, 30, 30) cm

Monsina Men's Pullover Schematic

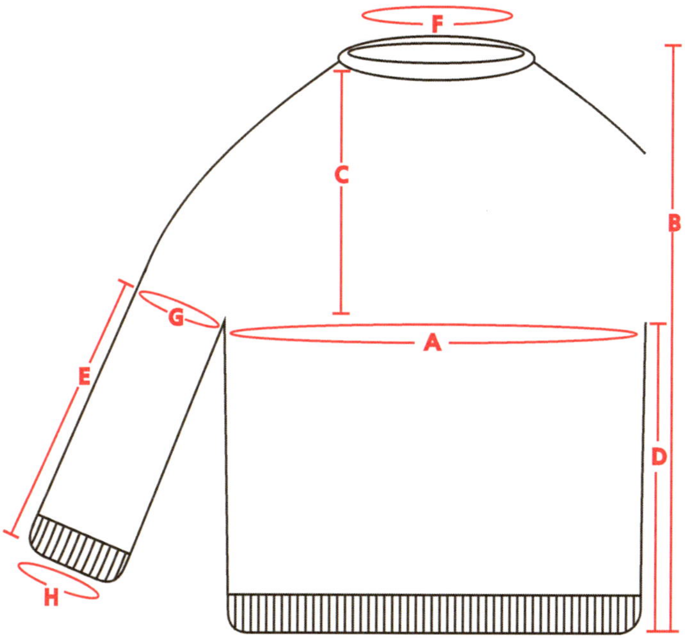

A CHEST CIRCUMFERENCE:
38½ (42¼, 47¼, 51, 55¼, 59) inches
96.5 (105.5, 118, 127.5, 138, 147.5) cm

B PULLOVER LENGTH:
24 (25, 25¾, 26½, 27½, 28¼) inches
60.5 (63, 65, 67, 69, 71.5) cm

C YOKE DEPTH:
10¾ (11¼, 11½, 11¾, 12¼, 12½) inches
27 (28, 29, 29.5, 30.5, 31.5) cm

D BODY LENGTH:
13¼ (13¾, 14¼, 14¾, 15¼, 15¾) inches
33.5 (35, 36, 37.5, 38.5, 40) cm

E SLEEVE LENGTH:
16¾ (17¾, 19, 20, 20½, 21) inches
42.5 (45, 48, 50.5, 52, 53) cm

F NECK CIRCUMFERENCE:
18 (19¾, 19¾, 21¼, 23, 23) inches
45 (49, 49, 53, 57.5, 57.5) cm

G UPPER ARM CIRCUMFERENCE:
13½ (14½, 15¾, 16¾, 18¼, 19¼) inches
33.5 (36.5, 39, 42, 45.5, 48) cm

H CUFF CIRCUMFERENCE:
9¾ (11, 11, 11, 12, 12) inches
24.5 (27.5, 27.5, 27.5, 30, 30) cm

Monsina (Men's Pullover)

Construction Notes

This garment is worked seamlessly in the round from the top down.

Directions for the Knitted Cast On and Jeny's Surprisingly Stretchy Bind Off, as well as other useful information, can be found in the Special Techniques section of the book.

The garter stitch neckband is worked flat, then the yoke is knit in the round with increases occurring before and after each band of stranded colorwork.

The yoke is then divided to work the body, with additional stitches cast on at the underarms, while the sleeve stitches are held separately.

The sleeves are worked from the upper arm down with stitches picked up from the cast-on edge at the underarms and are tapered with decreases below the elbow.

3x3 Ribbing is worked at the hem and the cuffs.

Yarn is held double-stranded throughout.

Stitch Patterns

3X3 RIBBING

Worked over a multiple of 6 sts; 1-rnd repeat.
Rnd 1: *K3, p3; rep from * around.
Rep Rnd 1 as directed.

Pattern Instructions

YOKE

Using Knitted cast-on method, CO 99 (108, 108, 117, 126, 126) sts using Color A. Do not join. Knit 8 rows flat. With RS facing, join in the rnd and pm to indicate EOR, being careful not to twist sts. Knit 2 rnds.

Work Rnds 1-7 of Chart 1 with Colors A, B, C and D, repeating to EOR. Cut Colors B, C and D. With Color A only, knit 1 rnd even. Knit 1 rnd, inc 1 (0, 0, 1, 0, 0) st(s). 100 (108, 108, 118, 126, 126) sts on needles. Cut Color A.

With Color E only, work Inc Rnd 1: *K2, M1; rep from * around. 150 (162, 162, 177, 189, 189) sts on needles. Knit 1 rnd, inc 3 (0, 0, 3, 0, 0) sts evenly. 153 (162, 162, 180, 189, 189) sts on needles.

Work Rnds 1-9 of Chart 2 with Colors E, F, G and H, repeating to EOR. Cut Colors, F, G and H. With Color E only, knit 1 rnd even. Knit 1 rnd, inc 1 (0, 0, 0, 1, 1) st(s). 154 (162, 162, 180, 190, 190) sts on needles. Cut Color E.

With Color A only, work Inc Rnd 2: *K2, M1; rep from * around. 231 (243, 243, 270, 285, 285) sts on needles. Knit 1 rnd, inc 3 (0, 0, 0, 3, 3) sts evenly. 234 (243, 243, 270, 288, 288) sts on needles.

Work Rnds 1-7 of Chart 1 with Colors A, B, C and D, repeating to EOR. Cut Colors B, C and D.

Project Overview (Men's Pullover)

SIZES

XS (S, M, L, XL, XXL) to fit chest circumference of 36" (40", 44", 48", 52", 56") [91.5 cm (101.5 cm, 112 cm, 122 cm, 132 cm, 142 cm)] with 2¼-3¼" [4-6 cm] of positive ease intended.

Shown in Size XL with 3¼" [6 cm] of positive ease.

FINISHED MEASUREMENTS

Chest Circumference: 38½" (42¼", 47¼", 51", 55¼", 59") [96.5 cm (105.5 cm, 118 cm, 127.5 cm, 138 cm, 147.5 cm)].

Pullover Length: 24" (25", 25¾", 26½", 27½", 28¼") [60.5 cm (63 cm, 65 cm, 67 cm, 69 cm, 71.5 cm)].

YARN

Ístex Einband: 100% Icelandic wool; 273 yds [250 m] per 1.75 oz [50 g] skein.

- Color A: 9142 Fuchsia; 2 skeins for all sizes.
- Color B: 9281 Sky Blue; 2 skeins for all sizes.
- Color C: 9028 Citron; 2 skeins for all sizes.
- Color D: 9044 Purple; 2 skeins for all sizes.
- Color E: 9277 Royal Blue; 2 (2, 2, 4, 4, 4) skeins.
- Color F: 1768 Pink; 2 skeins for all sizes.
- Color G: 1764 Vivid Green; 2 skeins for all sizes.
- Color H: 0851 White; 2 skeins for all sizes.
- Color I: 1761 Teal; 4 (4, 4, 6, 6, 6) skeins.
- Color J: 9128 Blush; 2 skeins for all sizes.
- Color K: 1762 Turquoise; 2 skeins for all sizes.
- Color L: 1769 Cherry; 2 skeins for all sizes.

NEEDLES

US #6 [4.0 mm], or size needed to obtain gauge;

- All sizes: 16" [40 cm], 24" [60 cm], 32" [80 cm], and 40" [100 cm] circular needles.

- Sizes XL-XXL: 60" [150 cm] circular needles.
- Optional: double-pointed needles for small-circumference knitting.

Note: Begin with the shortest circular needles and switch to longer lengths as needed while working the yoke. Use your preferred method of small-circumference knitting to work the sleeves.

NOTIONS

1 stitch marker (to indicate end of round).

2 short circular stitch holders or waste yarn (to hold live stitches for sleeves).

Blocking pins, if desired.

GAUGE

22 sts and 24 rnds = 4" [10 cm] in St st with yarn held double-stranded, after blocking.

With Color A only, knit 2 rnds. Cut Color A.

With Color I only, work Inc Rnd 3: *K3, M1; rep from * around. 312 (324, 324, 360, 384, 384) sts on needles.

Sizes XS and XL only:

Knit 1 rnd, dec 6 sts evenly. 306 (378) sts on needles.

All other sizes:

Knit 1 rnd, inc - (0, 18, 0, -, 12) sts evenly. - (324, 342, 360, - , 396) sts on needles.

Work Rnds 1-15 of Chart 3 with Colors G, H, I, J, K and L, repeating to EOR. Cut Colors G, H, J, K and L. With Color I only, knit 2 rnds. Cut Color I.

With Color A only, knit 2 rnds even. Work Rnds 1-7 of Chart 1 with Colors A, B, C and D, repeating to EOR. Cut Colors B, C and D.

With Color A only, knit 1 rnd even. Knit 1 rnd, dec 30 (24, 18, 12, 6, 0) sts evenly. 276 (300, 324, 348, 372, 396) sts on needles. Cut Color A.

With Color I only, knit 0 (2, 4, 6, 8, 10) rnds even.

BODY

Divide body and sleeves from yoke as follows:

With Color I only, *knit 86 (94, 104, 112, 120, 128) sts (front/back). Place next 52 (56, 58, 62, 66, 70) sts (sleeve) on circular stitch holder or waste yarn. Using Knitted cast-on method, CO 20 (22, 26, 28, 32, 34) sts for underarm. Rep from * once, then pm to indicate EOR. 212 (232, 260, 280, 304, 324) sts on needles.

Work in St st until body measures 10¼" (10¾", 11¼", 11¾", 12¼", 12¾") [26 cm (27.5 cm, 28.5 cm, 30 cm, 31 cm, 32.5 cm)], or 3" [7.5 cm] less than desired length to hem.

Work 3x3 Ribbing for 18 rnds. BO all sts loosely using Jeny's Surprisingly Stretchy bind-off method.

SLEEVES (MAKE 2)

Using preferred needles for small-circumference knitting, beg at center of underarm with RS facing, join Color I and pick up and knit 10 (11, 13, 14, 16, 17) sts from CO sts at underarm, pick up and knit 1 st in gap between body and sleeve, knit 52 (56, 58, 62, 66, 70) sleeve sts from circular stitch holder or waste yarn, pick up and knit 1 st between body and sleeve, then pick up and knit rem 10 (11, 13, 14, 16, 17) from underarm CO edge. 74 (80, 86, 92, 100, 106) sts on needles.

Join in the rnd and pm to indicate EOR, being careful not to twist sts. Knit 2 rnds.

Cut Color I. With Color K only, knit 3 rnds. With Color G, knit 1 rnd.

Cut Color G. With Color K only, knit 3 rnds.

Cut Color K. With Color I only, knit 6 rnds.

Cut Color I. With Color A only, knit 4 rnds.

Cut Color A. With Color C only, knit 3 rnds.

Cut Color C. With Color A only, knit 4 rnds.

Cut Color A. With Color E only, knit 5 rnds.

Cut Color E. With Color G only, knit 3 rnds.

Cut Color G. With Color E only, knit 5 rnds.

Cut Color E. With Color A only, knit 4 rnds.

Cut Color A. With Color C only, knit 3 rnds.

Cut Color C. With Color A only, knit 4 rnds.

Cut Color A.

With Color E only, work in St st and dec 1 st at beg and end of every 2nd rnd, 10 (10, 13, 16, 17, 20) times. 54 (60, 60, 60, 66, 66) sts on needles.

Work in St st until sleeve measures 13¾" (14¾", 16", 17", 17½", 18") [35 cm (37.5 cm, 40.5 cm, 43 cm, 44.5 cm, 45.5 cm)], or 3" [7.5 cm] less than desired length to cuff.

Work 3x3 Ribbing for 18 rnds. BO all sts loosely using Jeny's Surprisingly Stretchy bind-off method.

NECKBAND

Sew ends together. Fold neck-band in half and sew to the inside of the garment.

FINISHING

Weave in all loose ends with tapestry needle on the inside of the garment. Block to finished measurements.

See Pages 110 and 111 for charts.

Abbreviations

beg	beginning
BO	bind off
cn	cable needle
cnb	cable needle back
cnf	cable needle front
CO	cast on
dec	decrease
EOR	end of round
est	established
foll	following
inc	increase
k	knit
k1fb	knit 1 front and back increase
kwise	knitwise

k2tog	knit 2 together
LH	left-hand
M1	make 1 increase
M1L	make 1 left increase
M1R	make 1 right increase
p	purl
patt	pattern
pm	place marker
psso	pass slipped stitch over
pwise	purlwise
p3tog	purl 3 together
rem	remaining

rep	repeat
RH	right-hand
rnd(s)	round(s)
RS	right side
sl	slip
sl m	slip marker
ssk	slip, slip, knit
St st	stockinette stitch
st(s)	stitch(es)
tbl	through back loop
tfl	through front loop
WS	wrong side
wyif	with yarn in front
yo	yarn over

Special Techniques

Channel Island Cast On

This cast on can be worked to start a project where a sturdy, yet flexible edge is needed. It produces an even number of stitches, which makes it perfectly suited to 1x1 Ribbing. These directions presume familiarity with the Long Tail cast-on method.

Step 1: Measure out a tail that is twice the length needed for a Long Tail Cast On. Fold in half and make a slip knot where the two strands come together at the end of the yarn, leaving a short tail that will be woven in at the end. Place the slip knot on RH needle.

Step 2: Hold the yarn in sling-shot position with the single strand of working yarn over LH index finger. Take the double-strand tail and loop it twice around LH thumb counterclockwise.

Step 3: Reach RH needle behind single strand of yarn, as if making a yarn over.

Step 4: Insert needle tip up under the doubled tail on LH thumb.

Step 5: Reach over the top of the single strand and pull a loop through.

Step 6: Drop the yarn from LH thumb and pull on ends to tighten st.

Rep Steps 2-6 until the required number of sts have been cast on. Repeated sequence makes 2 sts: first st is a yarn over, second st is a knot.

On the first row or rnd of knitting, knit the knots and purl the yarn overs. At the end of the first row or rnd, treat the 2 strands of the slip knot as 2 sts.

Estonian Lace Bind Off

Step 1: Slip the first st on LH needle pwise.

Step 2: Knit the next st on LH needle.

Step 3: Slip the two sts on RH needle back to LH needle pwise.

Step 4: K2tog tbl.

Rep Steps 2-4 until 1 st remains.

Cut working yarn and pull up last loop to secure the end of the bound-off stitches.

Icelandic Bind Off

This bind off creates a crisp, clean edge that is also very flexible, making it a natural choice for neckbands, cuffs and hems.

Step 1: Knit the first st on LH needle.

Step 2: Slip this st pwise back onto LH needle.

Step 3: Insert tip of RH needle through the first st on LH needle pwise and then into second st on LH needle as if to knit.

Step 4: Wrap working yarn around RH needle and pull a new st through both stitches on LH needle, letting these stitches drop off LH needle. (1 st bound off)

Rep Steps 2-4 until 1 st remains.

Increase the size of the final stitch by pulling back on RH needle while holding stitches that had previously been bound off between LH thumb and index or middle finger. Once the diameter of the last stitch is about 3" [7.5 cm] long, cut this elongated stitch in the middle. Pull on working yarn with right hand to separate it from the stitch. All that now remains of this stitch is a 3" [7.5 cm] tail that needs to be woven in.

Thread this tail into a tapestry needle and weave it in by inserting the tip of the tapestry needle under both legs of the first stitch that was bound off at the beginning of the round and pulling the tail through. Then insert the needle from above between the legs of the stitch from which the tail emerged. Finally, pull the tail through the center of this stitch and weave it in on the wrong side of the work.

Jeny's Surprisingly Stretchy Bind Off

This bind off combines the classic simple bind off with a yarn wrap. It is especially useful for binding off ribbing in the round, as it creates hinges at the points where the ribbing changes between knit and purled stitches, making the bound-off edge suitably flexible. These instructions have been adapted from the article by Jeny Staiman in the Fall 2009 issue of Knitty in which this technique was introduced and from the YouTube video by Cat Bordhi in which it is demonstrated.

Every stitch on the LH needle is processed as described below as it is worked, depending on whether it was knit or purled in the previous round. Once two stitches have been processed and placed on the RH needle, the right stitch is passed over the left stitch and slipped off the RH needle to bind off.

To process a knit stitch: Work a reverse yo (wrap working yarn around RH needle in the opposite direction from the standard yo), knit first st on LH needle, insert tip of LH needle into yo and pass it over the st that was just knit and off RH needle.

To process a purl stitch: Work a standard yo (wrap working yarn around RH needle in the usual direction), purl first st on LH needle, insert tip of LH needle into yo and pass it over the st that was just purled and off RH needle.

The direction that the working yarn is wrapped when processing stitches is related to the usual way the working yarn is moved to the back or front between the needles when working a knit stitch after a purl or a purl stitch after a knit, respectively. When processing a stitch that is different from the one before, the working yarn is effectively moved to the back or front between the needles twice.

To bind off: Process each of the first two sts on LH needle, *with tip of LH needle pass right st over left st and slip it off RH needle, process next st on LH needle, rep from * until 1 st remains. (Once one stitch has been processed, the yarn over and the right stitch on RH needle can be passed over the stitch being processed and slipped off needle at the same time.)

Increase the size of the final stitch by pulling back on RH needle while holding stitches that had previously been bound off between LH thumb and index or middle finger. Once the diameter of the last stitch is about 3" [7.5 cm], cut this elongated stitch in the middle. Pull on working yarn with right hand to separate it from the stitch. All that now remains of this stitch is a 3" [7.5 cm] tail that needs to be woven in.

Thread this tail into a tapestry needle and weave it in by inserting the tip of the tapestry needle under both legs of the first stitch that was bound off at the beginning of the round and pulling the tail through. Then insert the needle from above between the legs of the stitch from which the tail emerged. Finally, pull the tail through the center of this stitch and weave it in on the wrong side of the work.

Kitchener Stitch

This method of grafting live stitches together requires an equal number of stitches on each of the two needles. It creates an invisible join that is well suited to underarm seams.

Step 1: Hold both needles together in left hand so that they are parallel and pointing to the right. The WS of the pieces to be grafted are held together and the RS of the work is facing outward. The yarn tail should be threaded though a tapestry needle and held to the right. Make sure that the working yarn is always held below both needles and that the yarn is always pulled through gently.

Step 2: Insert the tapestry needle through the first st on the front needle as if to purl and pull the yarn through. Leave first st on front needle.

Step 3: Insert the tapestry needle through the first st on the back needle as if to knit and pull the yarn through. Leave first st on back needle.

Step 4: On the front needle, insert the tapestry needle through the first st kwise and slip first st off front needle.

Step 5: Insert the tapestry needle through the next st on front needle as if to purl and pull the yarn through. Leave this st on front needle.

Step 6: On the back needle, insert the tapestry needle through the first st pwise and slip first st off back needle.

Step 7: Insert the tapestry needle through the next st on back needle as if to knit and pull the yarn through. Leave this st on back needle.

Rep Steps 4-7 until all sts have been worked, ending with Step 4 and Step 6. Adjust tension of grafted sts to match gauge of knitting as closely as possible.

Knitted Cast On

This cast on can be worked to start a project or to add stitches to an existing project. If adding stitches, begin with Step 2.

Step 1: Make a slip knot with working yarn and place it on needle. This will count as your first st. Hold this needle in left hand and an empty needle in right hand.

Step 2: Insert tip of RH needle into first st as if to knit, wrap working yarn around and pull through a new st.

Step 3: Twist RH needle so the two needles are side by side with points up. Insert tip of LH needle into new st on RH needle from bottom to top.

Step 4: Carefully remove tip of RH needle from new st and pull on working yarn with right hand to tighten new st on LH needle (1 st cast on).

Rep Steps 2-4 until the required number of sts has been cast on.

If starting a project, cast on required number of stitches then work first row of pattern, beginning with first stitch on LH needle (the last stitch cast on). Make sure that the original slip knot was included in the total number of cast-on stitches.

If adding stitches in the middle of a round, you must first turn work so that last stitch knit on RH needle becomes first stitch on LH needle. Cast on required number of stitches, turn work again so that last stitch cast on is now on RH needle, then continue working pattern round with next stitch on LH needle.

K1fb (Knit 1 Front and Back) Increase

Step 1: Knit the first st on LH needle tfl and leave st on LH needle.

Step 2: Knit the first st on LH needle again tbl and slip st off LH needle.

M1 (Make 1) Increase

Step 1: Create a backward loop around LH thumb and slip onto RH needle (1 st increased).

Step 2: On the next rnd, knit the new stitch tbl.

M1L (Make 1 Left) Increase

Step 1: Insert tip of LH needle from front to back under the strand of yarn between the next st on LH needle and the st just worked.

Step 2: Knit this strand tbl (1 st increased).

M1R (Make 1 Right) Increase

Step 1: Insert tip of LH needle from back to front under the strand of yarn between the next st on LH needle and the st just worked.

Step 2: Knit this strand tfl (1 st increased).

Picot Cast On

Step 1: CO 5 sts using knitted cast-on method.

Step 2: Knit the first 2 sts on LH needle.

Step 3: BO 1 st by passing right st over left st on RH needle and slipping it off needle.

Step 4: Knit the next st on LH needle.

Step 5: Rep Step 3.

Step 6: Slip the rem st on RH needle back to LH needle pwise.

Step 7: CO 4 sts using knitted cast-on method.

Step 8: Rep Steps 2-6.

Rep Steps 7 and 8 until the required number of sts have been cast on.

Provisional Cast On

These instructions have been adapted from an article in the Fall 2005 issue of Knitty by Theresa Vinson Stenersen.

This cast on can be worked with the cable from a spare circular needle or holder or with waste yarn. If using a spare needle or holder, substitute the word "cable" for "waste yarn" below.

Step 1: Make a slip knot with working yarn and place it on both tips of a circular needle. Hold the tips of needle, the tail end of working yarn and one end of waste yarn in right hand. Hold working yarn and the other end of waste yarn in left hand, with working yarn held above waste yarn (1 st cast on).

Step 2: Move working yarn in front of and under waste yarn, then in front of and over both tips of needle. End with working yarn held above waste yarn in left hand and tips of needle and new stitch held between RH thumb and index or middle finger (1 st cast on).

Rep Step 2 until the required number of sts have been cast on (including the original slip knot). End by wrapping working yarn in front of and under waste yarn and holding both ends of waste yarn in right hand.

Make sure that the number of stitches around waste yarn is the same as the number of stitches on the needle tips.

Carefully remove one tip of needle from stitches and turn work, holding the other tip of needle with stitches and waste yarn in left hand. Work first row of pattern, holding waste yarn at bottom of stitches between LH thumb and index or middle finger.

Short Row Shaping Using Yarn Overs

This method utilizes a yarn over at the end of each short row, rather than the more common wrap-and-turn. The yarn overs are later worked together with the adjacent stitches to eliminate gaps at the turns.

To create a yarn over on a knit row (RS): Knit to specified point, turn work so WS is facing, move working yarn to back between LH and RH needles, then around the RH needle to the front, ready to purl back in the opposite direction. This motion creates a yarn over that rests on the outside of the turning point.

To create a yarnover on a purl row (WS): Purl to specified point, turn work so RS is facing, bring working yarn to front between LH and RH needles, then around the RH needle to the back, ready to knit back in the opposite direction. This motion creates a yarn over that rests on the outside of the turning point.

When working St st in the rnd, all yarn overs will be hidden while working the first full rnd after completing the short rows back and forth.

To hide a yarn over created on a knit row (RS): Work to the yarn over on LH needle, then work it together with the next st as a k2tog.

To hide a yarn over created on a purl row (WS): Work to 1 st before the yarn over on LH needle, slip the stitch kwise, slip the yarn over pwise, then slip both back onto LH needle pwise and knit them together through the back loops.

Yarn Dominance

When working stranded colorwork with 2 colors, 1 color will appear to be slightly more dominant than the other color. This effect occurs because the strands of 1 color have to travel slightly farther than those of the other color. As a result, the stitches created by the yarn that travels the greater distance are a little tighter, which causes that color to recede into the background. The yarn that travels the shorter distance will be the dominant color.

Yarn dominance can also be explained by examining the wrong side of the fabric. The yarn that comes from below will be the dominant color and the yarn that lies on top will be the background color. To control this effect, always hold the yarn of the dominant color closer to the tips of the needles than the yarn of the background color.

When working stranded colorwork with more than 2 colors, the concept of relative dominance comes into play. Yarns should be assigned positions in relation to the other yarns in order to maintain consistency throughout the project. Colors will need to be ranked in order from most dominant to least dominant and their yarns should be held accordingly.

About the Author

Known primarily for his irreverent "Does a Bear Knit in the Woods?" from the early days of knitting blogs, Lars Rains maintains that everyone is creative enough to become a knitwear designer if they put in the time and effort necessary to master the craft.

His design work pushes the envelope by juxtaposing colors, yarn weights and different techniques in order to create new projects using his beloved Icelandic wool. Lars firmly believes that knitters should try to learn a little something new with each project.

Lars bought his first lopapeysa from his college roommate in 1989 and he still has it to this day. (It looked better on him anyway.) He learned how to knit because he originally thought that it would be cheaper to knit sweaters than to buy them. He knows better now, but that hasn't slowed him down at all. His early Lopi projects were primarily monochromatic and textured, but today he challenges knitters to make bolder, brighter and more daring choices in their color selections.

Having studied mathematics, music theory and criticism, film theory, gender studies and queer theory, these themes frequently crop up in his work in the most intriguing and playful ways. A retired New York City police officer, Lars now works as a special education teacher in Queens, New York and is always teaching, whether in the classroom or through his work as a designer and knitting instructor.

Lars enjoys studying languages in his down time - the more obscure, the better. An athlete in his younger days, lately he prefers to hibernate with his husband and their two dogs and simply stay on the couch and knit. His deep affection for the people in his life, his cheeky sense of humor, and his adventurous sense of color all shine through in his work. He can be found online at www.modernlopi.com and on Ravelry as ModernLopi.

Lightning Source UK Ltd.
Milton Keynes UK
UKRC01n0146060218
317421UK00003B/20
* 9 7 8 0 9 9 7 0 0 0 4 2 9 *